IS FUN

ASHUTOSH PANDEY

INDIA · SINGAPORE · MALAYSIA

Notion Press

Old No. 38, New No. 6
McNichols Road, Chetpet
Chennai - 600 031

First Published by Notion Press 2019
Copyright © Ashutosh Pandey 2019
All Rights Reserved.

ISBN 978-1-64650-864-8

Dedicated To

My students and readers of this book

CONTENTS

CHAPTER 1

INTRODUCTION

Programming is a technique to make the computer work according to our requirements. All software in the world is a program or collection of more than one program. A program may be defined as a set of code that is written to perform a specific task.

Programming involves solving problems by applying some logic. To write programs, we have to choose a programming language that allows us to write code and test them. It's up to us which programming language we choose as per our requirement. Examples of popular programming language are:

```
C, Java, C#, etc.
```

Why C?

C is one of the most popular programming languages of the world because of its simplicity, reliability, power and ease of use. It is a general purpose language meaning it can be used to write simple calculation programs, hardware interacting programs as well as for advanced programming (e.g. in mobile devices).

C got its name on the basis of previous languages which were A, B (there were lots of other programming languages before C).

C provides the base of whatever programming language you are going to use in the future. Writing programs in C does not need remembering many statements and keywords as compared to earlier programming languages.

C is an easy language to write and run programs put you need a lot of practice for sure.

History

C programming language was planned and invented in the early 1970s by Dennis M. Ritchie, an employee from Bell Labs (AT&T). He checked out the drawbacks of B language like it did not have data types, structures, etc.

During 1971–73, Dennis M. Ritchie turned the B language into the C language, keeping most of the B language syntax while adding data-types and many other changes. C language had a powerful mix of high-level functionality as well as the detailed features required to program an operating system. Hence, C became hugely popular among programmers and still is one of the most popular languages for starting programming.

What is programming?

Programming is the process of solving a problem with the help of a computer. We first analyze how to solve the problem and then write instructions that a computer understands. The computer then executes these instructions (called a program) and we get the result.

The first mistake most programmers do is they directly start thinking about how to write the program instead of solving the problem first. They should break the problem into steps (parts) first and then solve each step one by one.

> **Note**
>
> To become a good programmer, you need to create more and more programs.

Algorithm

An algorithm is a written document that contains the steps to solve a problem. For example, let us consider a problem in which we have to find big number from given two numbers. The algorithm for this can be written as:

1. Get two numbers from user.
2. Compare the two numbers and store bigger number.
3. Print the bigger number.
4. Finish.

Program

A program is a well-defined set of instructions that a computer executes to provide the desired result. A program is a collection of lines of text that represents instructions to the computer. A program is generally written in text form and need to be translated into machine code which computer can understand. After this, statements (lines of code) are executed one by one and we get the result.

Starting C

To start writing programs in **C**, we need a compiler and an editor.

Compiler is a tool which checks our program for errors and converts our code into machine code. If there are any errors in our program, it will highlight those errors.

An editor is a text editing software (e.g. Notepad) that is used to write our code.

Nowadays, a compiler and an editor comes in a combined form called an *IDE* (Integrated Development Environment) which provides various tools that help us to write the programs in an efficient manner. We can execute all the tasks related to a program from within the *IDE* itself.

Some of the popular *IDEs* are:

```
Netbeans, TurboC (old), Eclipse, etc.
```

Data types

First of all, what is data? Data is anything that is useful to us. For example, "The capital of India is New Delhi" is a data. Data may contain characters such as alphabets('a', 'm' etc.), numeric values(1, 2, 3 etc.), special characters('$', '@' etc.). For our own convenience, we can divide these various characters into categories. These categories are called *data types*.

For example, if "food" is data, then "vegetables", "fruits" etc. are data types.

How 'C' understand various characters?

There is a classification in **C** that differentiates characters or symbols we use in our daily life. These are:-

Integers	:	1, 4, -34, -41, 870 etc.
		(No decimals)
Floating values	:	3.4, -1.608, 0.002 etc.
		(Numbers with decimal)
Characters	:	'a', '$', '#', 'K', '4' etc.
		(Characters are enclosed within ' ')
Strings	:	"Hello", "India", "12345" etc.
		(Strings are group of characters and are enclosed in " ")

Note

In the above discussion, if you noticed, 4 is defined as an integer as well as character. The difference between these two is that we can perform all mathematical operations like addition, multiplication etc. on integer 4 whereas no calculation can be performed on a character 4.

Variables and Literals

Literals are values that we use in our program.

Example:

```
1, 20, -3, 45...        Integer literals

'a', 't', 'M', 'y'...   Character literals

"good", "Hello"...      String literals
```

While writing a program, we need to store these literals (values) for further use. For example, consider this simple math statement:-

```
x = 5
y = 4.5
```

Here *5* and *4.5* are literals whereas *x* and *y* are variables that are used to store these literals. In terms of programming, a variable is a name given to a computer's memory location in which some value is stored.

Data types in C

Before we use a variable to store values, we need to define the data type of the variable. A data type defines the type of value we want to use in our program. Following are the data types that are commonly used in **C**:-

int	To store integer values
short	To store small integer values
long	To store large integer values
unsigned int	To store positive integer values
float	To store values having decimal
double	To store large values having decimal
char	To store characters

Range & memory of data type

The range is defined as the minimum and maximum values that can be stored in a variable of a given data type. The range of a data type depends on the size it occupies in the memory. Following are the range and size in memory of common data types:-

Data Type	Size	Min. Value	Max. Value
short	2 bytes	-32768	32767
int	2 bytes	-32768	32767
long	4 bytes	-2147483648	2147483647
unsigned int	2 bytes	0	65535
unsigned long	4 bytes	0	4294967295
float	4 bytes	$-3.4 * 10^{38}$	$3.4 * 10^{38}$
double	8 bytes	$-1.7 * 10^{308}$	$-1.7 * 10^{308}$
char	1 byte	-128	127
unsigned char	1 byte	0	255

We don't have to remember the range of these data types. In chapter 3, we will learn how to calculate the range of data types.

Statements in C

Any line written in a **C** program normally terminates with a semi-colon (;). Such a line is called a *statement*. Examples of statements in **C** are:-

int a, b, c = 5;
float m;
b = c * 2;

Identifiers

The name we give to variables is called an *identifier*. So, in the following statements, names *graduate* and *salary* are identifiers:-

char graduate;
long salary;

How to declare variables in C?

Before using a variable to store values in it, we need to tell the compiler the type of data we are going to store in it i.e. we need to define the data type of the variable. A variable cannot store values of two different data types.

To declare a variable, we first write the data type of the value it is going to store and then we write the name of the variable.

Example:

int a;

The variable *a* in the above line is declared to store only integer values. The semi-colon (;) here specifies the end of the statement. Some other examples of declaring variables are:

float hra;
char graduate;
long salary;   etc.

The next statement declares two variables in a single line. Both variables can store floating values.

float b, c;

Rules for giving names to variables

We cannot give just any name to a variable; instead, there are some rules. These rules are as follows:

1. The first letter of the variable name should be an alphabet or underscore (_).
2. No commas or spaces are allowed in a variable name.
3. No special characters like #, @, etc. are allowed in a variable name.
4. We can use alphabets, digits and underscore (_) only in a variable name.
5. The name may contain upper case letters.

Consider the following variables names:-

int _age;   valid
int 4u;   invalid, first letter cannot be number
int employee salary;   invalid, there should not be any space in variable name
int employee_salary;   valid
int number32;   valid
int email@yahoo;   invalid, no special character like @ is allowed

Case sensitive C

C is a case sensitive language i.e. we need to care about the case(upper or lower) of an identifier. But we can give capital (upper case) or small letters to variables names (identifiers).

For example:-

int cannot be written as *Int* or *INT*.
Employee_Salary is valid name but cannot be used as *employee_salary*.

Assigning values to the variables

Values can be assigned to variables in two ways:-

1. Assign literal to a variable
2. Assign the value of a variable to another variable

In each case, the value to be stored is placed on the right side of = and the variable in which value is to be stored is placed on the left side of =.

It should be noted that the left side of = should always have a variable.

Example

int a, b;
a = 5;   literal 5 is stored in the variable
b = a;   value of variable *a* is stored in variable *b*

We can also assign values while initializing the variables. For example:

int a = 5;
int b = a;

Similarly, we can assign different values to different data types as:-

char c = '$', more = 'y';
double z = 4.56;
int j, k;
j = k = 5;   both *j* and *k* have the value 5

One thing that should be carefully noted that if you try to assign a float value into an integer, short or a long variable, the digits after the '.' will be removed. For example:

int x;
x = 4.56;

The value stored in *x* will be 4 and not 4.56 as the variable *x* can store only integer values. Similarly, if write a statement like:-

float x = 4;

The value of *x* will be 4.000000 instead of 4 as floating values must have a decimal and by default, each float value has 6 digits after decimal in **C**.

Keywords

Keywords are reserved words in **C** language that are meant to do some special work. For example, we have already seen the following **C** keywords:

int, float, short, long, char, double, unsigned

All these keywords are meant to define the data type of a variable. Thus the statement:-

float int;

that tries to declare a variable *int* of data type *float* is wrong because *int* is a **C** keyword and cannot be used to name variables.

Arithmetic statements

These statements are simple math statements that perform some calculations or assign value to a variable. Examples of arithmetic statements are:

```
int a;
a = 5;
a = 5 * 6 - 3 + 4;
```

It should be carefully noted that first all the calculations on the right side of the = are executed and then the resulting value is assigned to the variable *a*.

Operators & Operands

An operator is a symbol that indicates some calculation between one or more values (operands). For example, in the statement:-

```
a = b * 3;
```

```
* is multiply operator
= is assignment operator
a, b, 3 are operands
```

Following are some of the examples of operators and their result:-

```
int a = 4, b = 7, c;
c = a + b;
```

Here the values of *a* and *b* are added and the result 11 is stored in the variable *c*.

7/3	result = 2	The result is integer because both 7 and 3 are integers.
7/3.3	result = 2.121212	Floating result as 3.3 is double
7.2/3	result = 2.400000	Floating result as 7.2 is double

Note

C do not allow calculation on the left side of =. There should be only variable on the left side of the assignment operator. Thus the following statement is incorrect:-

```
4 = x;
```

Operator types

Following are the type of operators we are going to use in **C** language:

1. Arithmetic operators

For mathematical calculations:

```
/    %    *    +    -
```

2. Unary operators

Require single operand:

++ (Increment)   -- (Decrement)   sizeof()   (type)

3. Relational operators

Gives result as 0 (false) or 1 (true):

```
<   <=   >    >=   ==   !=
```

4. Logical operators

For logical operations – AND, OR, NOT:

```
&&       ||    !
```

5. Bitwise operators

To perform operations on bits:

```
&  |    <<   >>   ~    ^
```

6. Assignment operators

Used to assign values to the variables:

```
=    +=    -=    /=    *=    %=
&=        |=
<<=       >>=    ^=
```

The operators are also classified as follows:

Unary: Works on a single operand.
++x

Binary: Works on two operands.
a + 5

Ternary: Works on three operands.
x = y > 10 ? 20 : 30

Operator precedence

Operator precedence describes the order in which **C** executes operators i.e. when executing multiple operators in a single statement, which operator should be executed first and in which direction. The precedence for the arithmetic operators is as follows:-

(* / %) , (+ -)

If any or all of the above operators are placed in a single statement, then solve the statement as follows:-

1. From left to right, solve *, / or % whichever comes first.
2. Now from left to right, solve + or - whichever comes first.

Thus, we can say that *, /, % have the same precedence whereas +,- have the same precedence. Also *, /, % have higher precedence than +,-.

Example

```
int a;
a = 5 + 6 * 3 - 7 / 2 + 3;
```

Execution

a = 5 + 18 - 7 / 2 + 3;	from left to right, 6 * 3 is solved first.
a = 5 + 18 - 3 + 3	from left to right, 7 /2 is now solved which gives 3 (integer result)
a = 23 - 3 + 3	from left to right, 5 + 18 is solved
a = 20 + 3	from left to right, 23 - 3 is solved
a = 23	

Operator precedence chart

Operator Type	Operator	Associativity
Primary Expression Operators	() [] . -> expr++ expr--	left-to-right
Unary operators	* & + - ! ~ ++expr --expr (typecast) sizeof	right-to-left
Binary Operators	* / %	left-to-right
	+ -	
	>> <<	
	< > <= >=	
	== !=	
	&	
	^	
	|	
	&&	
	||	
Ternary Operator	? :	right-to-left
Assignment Operator	= += -= *= /= %= >>= <<= &= ^= |=	right-to-left
Comma	,	left-to-right

SOLVED QUESTIONS

Q.1. What is the assignment statement called while declaring a variable?

Ans. An assignment statement while declaring the variable is called the initialization statement.

Q.2. What to do you mean by swapping?

Ans. Interchanging value of variables is called swapping.

$a = 5$
$b = 6$

Using a third temporary variable, we can do swapping:

c = a	=>	c is 5 now
a = b	=>	a is 6 now
b = c	=>	b is 5 now

Q.3. Can we swap the value of two numbers without using a third variable?

Ans. Yes, this can be done as follows:

$a = 5$
$b = 6$

a = a + b;	=>	a is 11 now
b = a - b;	=>	b is 5 now
a = a - b;	=>	a is 6 now

Q.4. What is the difference between a compiler and an interpreter? Which one of these two **C** uses?

Ans. A compiler checks the whole program and shows the errors if any, whereas an interpreter checks the code line by line and stops on the very first line where it found the error. A compiler is generally fast in finding errors whereas an interpreter is slow but accurate in finding an error. **C** uses a compiler whereas languages like *Visual Basic* uses an interpreter.

Q.5. Are all the errors reported by the compiler correct?

Ans. The errors reported by a compiler are generally correct but sometimes one error in the program can cause other statements to produce an error.

Q.6. Is it true that all the expressions in **C** are solved from left to right?

Ans. Most of the **C** expressions are solved from left to right according to the operator precedence but some of the statements are executed from right to left also.

Q.7. What are keywords and what are the limitations on using them?

Ans. Keywords are predefined words in **C** that are used in programs. These keywords are reserved for specific use and we cannot modify them to use them for our own purpose.

Examples of keywords are:

int, main, float, char, etc.

Q.8. What are identifiers?

Ans. The names we give to variables, functions, etc. are called identifiers.

Q.9. What are literals?

Ans. The values we assign to variables are called literals. In the statement x=4, 4 is literal.

Q.10. What are the following symbols called?
()   {}   []   <>

Ans. () is called parenthesis

{} is called curly braces

[] is called square bracket

<> is called angular bracket or chevron

CHAPTER 2

LET'S WRITE PROGRAMS

Header Files

Each programming language have some rules to write programs and so does **C**. There are various symbols/characters that we write in our programs. Also, we declare various variables and assign values to them. How does the compiler know which values are right and which are wrong? For this, **C** has predefined files, called **header files**, which tells the compiler that the words or values used in the program are correct. A header file is included at the beginning of the program like this:-

```
#include<HeaderFileName.h>
```

Here *HeaderFileName* is the name of the header file that is to be included and *.h* is its extension that denotes a header. The most common and important header file that should be included in our program is *stdio.h*. This file can be included in our program as:-

```
#include<stdio.h>
```

std	stands for standard
i	stands for input
o	stands for output
h	stands for header

An introduction to function

A function is a named block of code that can be used anywhere as well as any number of times in the program. They are used to make program short and efficient. An example of a function is:

```c
int square(int n)
{
    return n*n;
}
```

The above function will receive an integer value and returns the square of that number. Since it returns an integer value, there is *int* (return type) on the left side of the function name.

This function can be used in a program like this:

```
int result = square(5);
```

On this statement, the function will be executed and the value of *result* will be set to 25.

We will learn about functions in detail in the coming chapters.

main()

After adding the header file(s), the program coding starts by writing the function *main()*. All the actual coding is done in the body of this function. The function *main()* starts with the starting curly bracket { and ends with the closing curly bracket }. Thus a basic program structure looks like this:

```
#include<stdio.h>

int main()
{
    ....................................
    ...program statements...
    ....................................
    return 0;
}
```

When we try to compile the program, the compiler first searches the function *main()* from where the program execution begins. Then it goes in a downward direction to check the statements written in the *main()* one by one.

Function *main()* returns 0 at the end, to tell the execution environment that program completed successfully. Any other value returned is generally considered as a status code representing type of problem in the program.

Comments

Comments are statements that are used for creating notes about other statements. Comments are used by programmers to add explanation to the code. Comments are ignored by the compiler during compilation and not added to compiled code. With the help of comments, we can write a hint about what a part of the program is doing.

A comment starts with symbols /* and ends with the symbols */. For example:

```
/* The next line will declare an integer */
int a;
```

Here the comment will be ignored by the compiler and the statement *int a;* will be executed. A comment can be written on more than one line like this:-

```
/* The next line will declare an integer
   It also assigns the value 5 to the integer variable */
int a = 5;
```

Output to screen

We can send the output of the program (text, numbers, etc.) to the computer's screen with the help of the function *printf()*. This function prints whatever is given inside its () to the compute's screen.

Example:

```
printf("Hello world");
```

This statement will print the line *Hello world* on the computer's screen.

Our first program

First of all, you should install an IDE (Integrated Development Environment) so that we can develop our **C** programs easily. An IDE provides various tools to develop, compile and execute our programs. It also provides help to various functions provided by **C**.

One of the most popular IDEs are *Netbeans* & *TurboC*. Start it and create a new C file using *File->New* menu option. Write the following statements in the program:-

```
#include<stdio.h>

int main()
{
    printf("Hello World");
    return 0;    /* tell operating system, program finished without errors */
}
```

Now compile the program by selecting compile from the compile menu. If you are using TurboC IDE, this can be done by pressing *Alt F9* keys. The compiler will show a small box saying 0 warnings and 0 errors. Now you can run the program to see the output by selecting Run from the Run menu or by pressing the *Ctrl F9* keys. To see the result screen, select *User Screen* from the Run menu or press *Alt F5* keys.

Explanation:

After running the program, the compiler first reaches the function *main()*. Then it prints the text *Hello World* on the output screen and finally, the last return statement tells the environment that program finished without errors. Comments are used only to mark what a function is doing and is simply ignored by the compiler.

Printing values of variables

To print the value of a variable, we have to tell the *printf()* function about the data type of the variable whose value is to be printed.

Let us check out some *printf()* statements:-

```
int a = 5;

/* This statement will print a on the output screen */
printf("a");

/* This statement will print 5 i.e. the value of variable a on the screen */
printf("%d", a);

char currency = '$';
int age = 25;
float salary = 5000.00;

/* This will print values of all three variables */
printf("%d  %f  %c", age, salary, currency);
```

Here is a list of all the format specifiers we can use in our program.

Specifier	Purpose
%i or %d	To print integer values
%u	To print positive integers (unsigned)
%o	To print octal numbers
%x or %X	To print hexadecimal numbers
%f, %g, %G	To print float or double values
%e, %E	To print float or double values in exponent form
%c	To print character
%s	To print string
%4d	Total 4 spaces to print integer value, right aligned
%-4d	Total 4 spaces to print integer value, left aligned

Let us write two programs together to understand how it works:-

Program# 1 - 2

```
#include<stdio.h>              #include<stdio.h>

int main()                     int main()
{                              {
    int a = 5;                     int a = 5;
    printf("a");                   printf("%d", a);
    return 0;                      return 0;
}                              }
```

Here is a comparison between the two programs that try to print the value of variable *a*.
The output of the left program will be *a*
The output of the right program will be *5*

We can clearly see that if we simply write the name of the variable in the *printf()* function, it is assumed as a character and printed as it is. In the second case, we first write the format specifier of the data type of the variable *a* which is *int* in this case. Then we write the comma and then the name of the variable whose value is to be printed.

Let us see one more example:-

Program# 3

```
#include<stdio.h>

int main()
{
    int a = 5;
    float b = 5.6;
    char m = '$';

    printf("Integer = %d, Float = %f, Character = %c", a, b, m);

    return 0;
}
```

Result:

Integer = 5, Float = 5.600000, Character = $

When the *printf()* function encounters *%d,* it goes to the variable names list and finds *a* first and prints its value. It then checks *%f* and again moves to the variable names list. It finds *b* as the next variable and prints its value. Similarly, the value of variable *m* is printed.

Program# 4

Perform common mathematical operations on two integer variables.

```c
#include<stdio.h>

int main()
{
    int a = 7, b = 3;

    printf("%d ", a + b);
    printf("%d ", a - b);
    printf("%d ", a * b);
    printf("%d ", a / b);
    printf("%d ", a % b);

    return 0;
}
```

Compile and run this program. The output should be:-
10   4   21   2   1

> **Note**
>
> It should be noted carefully that if you are declaring variables in a program, they should be placed before all other statements in the function.

Let us write one more program that will calculate simple interest. The formula for calculating simple interest compounded annually is:-

SimpleInterest = Principal * Rate * Time / 100;

Program# 5

Calculate simple interest.

```c
#include<stdio.h>

int main()
{
    float simple_interest, principal, rate, time;

    principal = 4000;          /* 4000 Rs. */
    rate = 6.5;                /* 6.5% */
    time = 2;                  /* 2 years */

    simple_interest = principal * rate * time / 100;
    printf("Simple interest is %f", simple_interest);

    return 0;
}
```

Compile and run this program. The output should be:-
520.000000

Good programming style

A program must be readable. Once you create your program, others should be able to understand what the program is doing.

1. Press enter and tab key after each {
2. Give a gap of one line after declaring variables in the program
3. Use comments in front or before the statements that are hard to understand.
4. Give proper names to the variables.

For example, to store the age of an employee, use variable name *emp_age* instead of *a* or *ag*.

Input in C

Till now we have set the values of the variables ourselves. But what the purpose of an actual program is that you write it, compile it and someone else uses it. When some other user uses your program, they may want to give their own values to the variables. These values are entered by the user during runtime (i.e. after running the program) and are stored in appropriate variables for further use.

In **C**, we can read values from the user by using the function *scanf()*. This function checks for the type of input value and the variable to which this value is to be assigned. A simple *scanf()* function can be written like this:-

```
scanf("%format", &variable);
```

Example:

```
int a;
```

```
/* Ask the user to enter some value */
```

```
printf("Enter a number ");
```

```
scanf("%d", &a);
```

Here *scanf()* function first checks the type of input (which is an integer here). To read an integer value, we have used the format specifier *%d*. It then assigns (stores) the value entered by the user in the variable *a*. The address operator & (ampersand) should be placed before the name of the variable in the body of the function *scanf()*.

Let us write a program that will use the function *scanf()* to read values from the user.

Program# 6

Calculate the sum of two numbers entered by the user.

```
#include<stdio.h>

int main()
{
    int a, b, c;

    printf("Enter first number : ");
    scanf("%d", &a);              /* Store first value in variable a */

    printf("Enter second number : ");
    scanf("%d", &b);              /* Store second value in variable b */

    c = a + b;

    printf("%d + %d = %d", a, b, c);

    return 0;
}
```

Compile and run this program. Let the two numbers entered by the user are 5 and 6. The output should be:-

5 + 6 = 11

In the last *printf()* function, the first *%d* prints the value of variable *a*, second *%d* prints the value of the variable *b* and the third *%d* prints the value of variable *c*.

> **Note**
>
> It is not necessary to use *scanf()* after each *printf()* function. *scanf()* is used only when we want to read some value from the user whereas *printf()* is used only when we want to show something to the user on the output screen.

Escape sequences

Escape sequences are the characters that are not printed when used but provide help in formatting the output on the screen. These are always started with a backslash \. Commonly used escape sequences are:-

Character	Escape sequence
bell(alert)	\a
backspace	\b
horizontal tab	\t
newline	\n
carriage(enter key)	\r
null	\0 etc.

Let us write a program to see the use of the above escape sequences.

Program# 7

Demonstrate the use of escape sequences.

```c
#include<stdio.h>

int main()
{
   printf("Hello\bWorld");
   printf("\nHow\nare you");
   printf("\nC is\tgood");

   return 0;
}
```

Compile and run this program. The output should be:-

```
HellWorld
How
are you
C is good
```

Explanation:

\b deletes the *o* of *Hello* as a normal backspace key does.
\n moves the text to be printed after it on the next line.
\t makes *good* to be printed after a tab stop.

What if we want to print \n,\ or' on the output screen?
Here is how we can do this:

```
printf("\\n");          Prints \n
printf("\\");           Prints \
printf("\' ");          Prints '
```

Thus, we have placed a backslash before each escape sequence so that it actually gets printed and not work in their usual way.

ASCII chart

Every character/number in **C** has a particular integer value through which it is identified. This integer value is called *ASCII (American Standard Code for Information Interchange)* value of that character or number. The ASCII values range from 0 to 255. Following is a table showing characters and their ASCII values:-

We can print ASCII code of any character in **C** with the help of *printf()* function like this:-

```
printf("%d", 'A');      Prints 65
printf("%d", 'B');      Prints 66

printf("%d", 'a');      Prints 97
printf("%d", 'b');      Prints 98

printf("%d", '0');      Prints 48
printf("%d", '1');      Prints 49
```

Similarly, we can print the character at a particular ASCII value as:-

```
printf("%c", 43);        Prints +
printf("%c", 65);        Prints A
```

Formatting in Input/Output

While getting input from the user or sending output on the screen, we can set limitations or formatting on the input/output values. Following are some examples that demonstrates formatting in *printf()*:-

> **Note**
>
> Write all below statements in function *main()* to compile and run.

Example:

```
1. int a;
   printf("Enter a number : ");
   scanf("%3d", &a);
   printf("Entered value is %d", a);
```

The *scanf()* function here restricts the input to be of 3 digits only. Hence, if the user enters the value 12345, the value stored in the variable *a* will be 123.

```
2. int a;
   printf("Enter a number : ");
   scanf("%d", &a);
   printf("%5d", a);
```

Let the user enters the value 123. In this example, while sending the value of the variable *a* to the output screen, first 5 spaces will be created and then 123 is printed in that space right justified. Thus there will be two blank spaces on the left side of 123 in the output. If the user enters 5 or more digits, the output will be normal.

```
3. int a;
   printf("Enter a number : ");
   scanf("%d", &a);
   printf("%-5d", a);
```

This time 5 spaces will again be created but the value will be printed left justified.

```
4. float a;
   printf("Enter a float value : ");
   scanf("%f", &a);
   printf("%7.2f", a);
```

In this example, if the user enters 1234.567, the output will be 1234.56 which will be right justified. This is because; *%7.2f* will set a total of 7 printing spaces including the decimal. Also, it will allow only two digits after the decimal.

```
5. float a;
   printf("Enter a float value : ");
   scanf("%f", &a);
   printf("%0.2e", a);
```

In this example, the output will contain exponent notation and 2 places after the decimal. Thus, if the user enters 45, the output will be 4.50e+01.

Constants

A constant is something that does not change. In **C**, we can declare identifiers whose value can't be changed. A constant in **C** can be defined by the keyword *define* like this:-

```
#define constant_name Value
```

Program# 8

Demonstrate the use of constant values.

```
#include<stdio.h>

#define PI 3.142

int main()
{
    float radius, area;

    printf("Enter the radius of the circle : ");
    scanf("%f", &radius);

    area = PI * radius * radius;
```

```
    printf("The area of the circle is %f", area);

    return 0;
}
```

Here we set the value of the constant named *PI* to 3.142. Thus, whenever we use the name PI in the program, 3.142 will be inserted in its place.

Also if we try to write a statement like:-

PI = 4;

The compiler will flash an error message telling that we can't modify the value of a constant identifier.

SOLVED PROBLEMS

Q.1. Can we scan values of different data types in a single *scanf()* function?

Ans. Yes, look at the following statements:-

```
int a;  float b;  char m;
printf("Enter an integer, a float and a character value : ");
scanf("%d %f %c", &a, &b, &m);
printf("Character = %c, Integer = %d, Float = %f", m, a, b);
```

Q.2. What happens when we enter a value that goes beyond the range of that data type?

Ans. Look at the following statements:-

```
int a = 300 * 300 / 300;
```

The expression is executed from left to right. Thus, 300 * 300 is executed first which gives the result 90000. But this value is greater than the maximum permissible number 32767 of an integer data type.

Whenever the compiler encounters such a situation, it turns to the negative side i.e. -32768. It then counts 90000 in the range -32768 to 32767 in a circular way. In our problem, after reaching 32767 it moves to negative side.

The value left to complete counting 90000 is 90000–32768 = 57232. Now it moves from -32768 to 0. The value left for counting is 57232–32768 = 24464. It moves from 1 to 24464 and finds that this value lies in the range of the integer data type. Hence the statement becomes:-

```
int a = 24464 / 300
```

which will give 81 as integer values don't have decimal.

Q.3. What will be the result of the following expression?
```
300 / (300 * 300)
```

Ans. The result will be 0. Here, the expression within the () will be solved first giving:-

300 / 24464 = 0.012262 and hence 0.

Q.4. What are strings? How can we initialize and use strings?

Ans. A string is simply collection of characters. Examples of string are "India", "Shiva" etc. Strings don't have a data type of their own. They are implemented with the help of arrays of characters which we will see in upcoming chapters.

Q.5. What is the meaning of the following statements?

```
int a;
a = printf("Hello reader, you are so valuable");
printf("%d", a);
```

Ans. The printf() function returns the number of characters it prints. Here it returns 32 including spaces which will be stored in the variable **a**.

Q.6. What is the meaning of the following statements?

```
int a, b;
float c, d;
char m;
a = scanf("%d %f %f %c", &a, &b, &c, &d, &m);
printf("%d", a);
```

Ans. The scanf() function returns the number of values it is scanning. Here it returns 5 which is stored in the variable *a*.

Q.7. What is the meaning of the following statements?

```
int a, b, c = 6, d;
a = b = c = d = c = c + 5;
```

Ans. The above expression is solved as follows:-

```
c = c + 5    gives c = 11
d = c        gives d = 11
c = d        gives c = 11
b = c        gives b = 11
a = b        gives a = 11
```

Q.8. What is the meaning of the following statements?

```
a = printf("Hello") * printf("Bye");
printf("%d", a);
```

Ans. Read Q.5. first. The above statement looks like:-

```
a = 5 * 3
```

Hence, the output will be 15.

CHAPTER 3

WORKING WITH BITS

Number system

A number system defines how different numbers can be represented and used. Following are the commonly used number systems:-

1. Decimal number system

We use numbers daily for various mathematical calculations. The numbers we use are:-

0 1 2 3 4 5 6 7 8 9

All other numbers are generated by using a combination of the above numbers. All the above numbers belong to the decimal number system where *dec* means 10. We have 10 different numbers in decimal number system with the help of which we can create any number. That is why we say that the base of this number system is 10.

Any number can be written according to its base. Let us look at the following example:-

Example:

517 is a normal number. This number can be written like this:-

$5 * 10^2 + 1 * 10^1 + 7 * 10^0 = 517$

Similarly, we can write any number using base 10 like this:

......	10^5	10^4	10^3	10^2	10^1	10^0		
	*	*	*	*	*	*		
				2	1	3	=	213
			1	0	2	6	=	1026

2. Octal number system

Oct means 8, so this number system has 8 different numbers i.e. the base of this number system is 8. The numbers allowed in this number system are:-

0 1 2 3 4 5 6 7

All the numbers in this number system can be generated with the help of above 8 numbers.

Example:

0341 (octal number)

This number is not equivalent to 341 of decimal number system. We have to convert it to see what number it represents in decimal number system. 0 before a number denotes that the number is an octal number.

Let us now convert this octal number (0341) into decimal number value.

$$\dots\dots 8^5 \quad 8^4 \quad 8^3 \quad 8^2 \quad 8^1 \quad 8^0$$
$$* \quad * \quad * \quad * \quad * \quad *$$
$$3 \quad 4 \quad 1$$

$3 * 8^2 + 4 * 8^1 + 1 * 8^0 = 225$ (decimal number)

To check, we will convert this decimal number value back to octal value. Divide the number by 8 until we get 0 as the remainder.

```
8 |    225
8 |     28    1
8 |      3    4
         0    3      remainders
```

Read the remainder from bottom to top and we get the result 0341. 0 is added to show that this number belongs to the octal number system.

We can print octal equivalent of a decimal number in **C** with the help of *printf()* function and *%o* format specifier. An example is:-

```
printf("%o", 225);
```

Similarly, to print decimal equivalent of an octal number, write:-

```
printf("%d", 0341);
```

3. Hexadecimal number system

This number system has 16 different numbers i.e. the base of this number system is 16. These numbers are:-

0 1 2 3 4 5 6 7 8 9 a b c d e f

Here a = 10, b = 11, c = 12, d = 13, e = 14, f = 15

Hexadecimal numbers has *0x* as prefix. An example of hexadecimal number is *0x2df*.

Let us look at an example that converts a hexadecimal number *0x2df* into its decimal equivalent:-

$$\ldots\ldots 16^5 \quad 16^4 \quad 16^3 \quad 16^2 \quad 16^1 \quad 16^0$$
$$* \qquad * \qquad * \qquad * \qquad * \qquad *$$
$$\qquad\qquad\qquad\qquad 2 \qquad d \qquad f$$

$$2 * 16^2 + 13 * 16^1 + 15 * 16^0 = 735 \text{ (decimal number)}$$

Here we have replaced *d* with *13* and *f* with *15*.

Decimal numbers can be converted to hexadecimal numbers in the same way as we have converted decimal numbers to octal numbers. Here is an example:-

```
16 |   735
16 |   45      15 = f
16 |   2       13 = d        remainders
        0       2
```

Read the remainder from bottom to top and we get the result is 0x2df.

Decimal numbers can be printed into hexadecimal numbers in **C** with the help of *printf()* function and the format specifier *%x* like this:-

```
printf("%x", 735);
```

Similarly, to print decimal value of a hexadecimal number, we can write:-

```
printf("%d", 0x2df);
```

Note

Case does not matter while writing the hexadecimal number. Hence, 2df can also be written as 2DF.

4. Binary number system

This is the number system that our computer understands. Binary means 2, hence this number system has only two numbers 0 and 1. Thus, the base of the binary number system is 2.

The numbers 0 and 1 are called *bits* in the binary number system. Each number in binary number system can be generated with the help of these two numbers.

We can convert a decimal number into its binary equivalent like this:-

```
2 |   42
2 |   21    0
2 |   10    1
2 |    5    0      remainders
2 |    2    1
2 |    1    0
        0    1
```

Read from bottom to top and we get the result $(101010)_2$.

Now to convert a binary number into decimal number, we do:-

2^6	2^5	2^4	2^3	2^2	2^1	2^0
*	*	*	*	*	*	*
	1	0	1	0	1	0

$1 * 25 + 0 * 24 + 1 * 23 + 0 * 22 + 1 * 21 + 0 * 20 = 73$ (decimal number value)

True and False

Every condition has one of the values, true or false. For example, "Is the road ahead blocked?". This question has answer *true* if the road is blocked and *false* if the road is not blocked.

In **C**, false is represented by 0 whereas any non-zero value is assumed true. **C** itself returns 1 for true and 0 for false.

Operations on bits

Following are the operations on bits that are used most commonly in **C**:-

1. AND (&&)

This operator takes two bits as input and produces one bit as a result according to the following rule:-

Input1	Input2	Output
0	0	0
0	1	0
1	0	0
1	1	1

If any input is 0, the output will be 0.

Example:

int k = 3 && 0;   Result :   k = 0

int i = 1, j = 1, k;
k = i && j;   Result :   k = 1

int i = 5, j = -14, k;
k = i && j;   Result: k = 1

The AND operator will treat any non-zero value as 1.

2. OR (||) (Pipe Operator)

This operator takes two bits as input and produces one bit as a result according to the following rule:-

Input1	Input2	Output
0	0	1
0	1	1
1	0	1
1	1	1

If any input is 1, the output will be 1.

Example:

int k = 3 || 0;   Result :   k = 1

int i = 0, j = 0, k;
k = i || j;   Result :   k = 0

int i = 5, j = -14, k;
k = i || j;   Result: k = 1

3. NOT (!)

This operator takes one bit as input and produces an inverted bit as output. Hence, if the input bit is 1, the output will be 0 whereas if the input bit is 0, the output will be 1.

Input	Output
1	0
0	1

Example:

int k = !25;   Result :   k = 0

int i = 10 % 5;
k = !i;   Result: k = 1

4. Bitwise AND (&)

This operator takes two binary numbers as input and produces a resultant binary number as output by applying AND (&&) operation to each bit of the binary numbers. If the number of bits in the input binary numbers are not the same, then add 0s to the left side of the binary number which has a lesser number of bits. Let us look at an example:

Example:

int i, j = 23, k = 10;
i = j & k;

Steps: 1.   j = 23 (decimal)   j = 10111 (binary)
              k = 10 (decimal)   k = 1010 (binary)

   2.   i = 23 & 10   is actually (10111) & (01010)

Here we have added one 0 to the left of the binary number 1010 to make the number of bits equal of both the binary numbers.

   3.   10111
         &&   01010
                00010 = 2

Result: i = 2

5. Bitwise OR (|)

This operator takes two binary numbers as input and produces a resultant binary number as output by applying OR (||) operation to each bit of the binary numbers.

Example:

int i, j = 23, k = 10;

i = j | k;

Steps: 1.   j = 23 (decimal)   j = 10111 (binary)
              k = 10 (decimal)   k = 1010 (binary)

   2.   i = 23 | 10   is actually (10111) || (1010)

   3.   10111
         || 01010
                11111 = 31

Result: i = 31

6. One's complement operator (~)

This operator takes a binary number as input and inverts every bit of the input number (converts 0 to 1 and 1 to 0). This is generally used with hexadecimal number system.

Example:

int i = 0x1a, k;

k = ~i;

i = 0000 0000 0001 1010

k = 1111 1111 1110 0101

Result: k = 0xffe5

7. Exclusive OR (^)

This operator takes two binary numbers as input and produces a resultant binary number as output by applying the following operation on each bit of the binary numbers:

If both input bits are the same, the result will be 0 and if the input bits are different, the result will be 1.

Input 1	Output	Input2
0	0	0
0	1	1
1	0	1
1	1	0

Example:

int k = 5;   k = 101 (binary)

j = k ^ 7;   7 = 111 (binary)

```
    101
^   111
    010 = 2
```

Result: j = 2

8. Left shift operator (<<)

This operator shifts the bits of a binary number to the left side and adds 0 to the right side. This operation can also be taken as if we are multiplying the number by 2 for each left shift.

Example:

int i = 17, k;

i = 10001 (binary)

k = i << 3;   i << 3 = 10001000

Result: k = 136

This operation can also be taken as:

k = 17 * 2 * 2 * 2

k = 136

9. Right shift operator(>>)

This operator shifts the bits of a binary number to the right side. The shifted bits are lost from the binary number. This operation can also be taken as if we are dividing the number by 2 for each right shift.

Example:

i = 10001 (binary) or 17 (decimal)

k = i >> 2;   i >> 2 = 100 (binary) or 4 (decimal)

Result: k = 4

This operation can also be taken as:

k = (17 / 2) / 2

k = 4

Binary arithmetic operations

1. Binary addition

Numbers are added in binary form with the following rules:

1. Each bit of the first number is added to the corresponding bit of the second number.
2. 0 + 0 = 0   carry = 0
3. 0 + 1 = 1   carry = 0
4. 1 + 0 = 1   carry = 0
5. 1 + 1 = 0   carry = 1

Example:

$(11010)_2 + (110)_2 \quad => \quad 26 + 6$

```
    1111          carry
    11010
+   00110
    ----------
   100000
```

Result: $(100000)_2 \quad => \quad 32$

2. Binary subtraction

Numbers are subtracted in binary form with the following rules:

1. Each bit of the second number is subtracted from the corresponding bit of the first number from right to left.
2. 0 - 0 = 0   borrow = 0
3. 0 - 1 = 1   borrow = 1
4. 1 - 0 = 1   borrow = 0
5. 1 - 1 = 0   borrow = 0

Example:

$(11010)_2 - (110)_2 \quad => \quad 26 - 6$

```
      1           borrow
    11010
 -  00110
    ----------
    10100
```

Result: $(10100)_2 \quad => \quad 20$

3. Binary multiplication

Numbers are multiplied in binary form in similar style as we multiply in decimal number system. Here are the rules:

1. Each bit of the second number is multiplied with all other bits of first number
2. After multiplication, bits are added to get result
3. 1 x 1 = 1
4. 1 x 0 = 0 x 1 = 0 = 0 x 0

```
  11010                    =>       26 x 6
  x 110
  ---------
  00000
  11010
 11010
 -----------
10011100
```

Result: $(10011100)_2$ =>   156

4. Binary division

Binary division can be done in the same way as we do decimal division. Here we will use binary multiplication and binary subtraction to obtain the result.

Example:

$(11000)_2 / (110)_2$ 24/6

```
              100      =>     Quotient = (100)_2   i.e.    4
 110       11000
             110
             000
             000
              000
              000
               0      =>     Remainder = 0
```

SOLVED PROBLEMS

Q.1. Multiply a number by 2^5 without using *, +,/or - operator.

Ans. This can be done by using the left shift operator '<<'.

```
int a = 3;
a = a << 5;    /* same as a * 2⁵ */
```

Q.2. Give the result of the following expression:-

```
int a = -1, b = 5, c;
c = ++a && ++b;
printf("%d %d %d", a, b, c);
```

Ans. 0 5 0

What happened to ++b? Here is the trick. There is an AND operation between *a* and *b*. The rule is if any input of the && operator is 0 (i.e. false), the result will be 0. Here ++a gives 0, which means one of the inputs of && is 0 and hence it does not matter what the second input is. Thus, ++b never gets executed.

Q.3. Give the result of the following expression:-

```
int a = 1, b = -1, c;
c = a-- || ++b;
printf("%d %d %d", a, b, c);
```

Ans. 0 -1 1

Here again, if any of the input of the OR operator is true (i.e. non-zero), the result will be 1. Here the value of variable *a* remains 1 as there is a post-decrement operator *a*-- which should be executed after this statement. Since one input of the || operator is true, it does not care about the second input and again ++*b* never get executed.

Q.4. Give the result of the following expression:-

```
int a = 4, b = 3, c = 2, d;
d = --a & --b + c << 2;
printf("%d %d %d %d", a, b, c, d);
```

Ans. 3 2 2 0

The value of *a*, *b* and *c* should be clear. In the given statement, operator precedence comes into play. The precedence of arithmetic operators is greater than bitwise operator. The precedence of the left shift operator is greater than bitwise AND operator. Hence, the given expression is solved as follows:

d = 3 & 2 + 2 << 2;
d = 3 & 4 << 2;
d = 3 & 16;
d = 0;

Q.5. What are bitwise assignment operators?

Ans. Here are the bitwise assignment operators:

a &= b;	which is same as	a = a & b;
a |= b;	which is same as	a = a | b;
a ^= b;	which is same as	a = a ^ b;
a <<= b;	which is same as	a = a << b;
a >>= b;	which is same as	a = a >> b;

These operators are used to assign the result of some bitwise expression into a variable that is taking part in the bitwise expression (which is *a* here).

Q.6. How can we get the size of a data type?

Ans. Size of a data type can be found with the help of *sizeof()* operator. For example:

```
printf("Size of integer is %d", sizeof(int));
printf("\nSize of float is %d", sizeof(float));
printf("\nSize of character is %d", sizeof(char));
```

Q.7. What is masking?

Ans. Masking is a process in which a given pattern of bits is converted into another pattern by using bitwise operation. The first bit pattern is the original bit pattern and the second bit pattern called *mask* is the group of bits with the help of which we want to get the desired pattern.

Let us look at the following example:

Let we want to get the 2 leftmost bits and 3 rightmost bits of a binary number. We can use a mask which will have 2 leftmost and 3 rightmost bits as 1 and we will perform the bitwise & operation.

Let a = 100100110011

mask = 110000000111

Result = a & mask

```
      100100110011
&     110000000111
      100000000011
```

Hence, in the resulting binary number, we have 2 leftmost and 3 rightmost bits of the binary number *a*.

Similarly, if we want that 5 left bits of a given binary number to become 1, we can do the masking like this:-

Let a = 100100110011

mask = 000000011111

Result = a | mask

```
      100100110011
&     000000011111
      100100111111
```

Q.8. What is the output of the following:-

```
int a = 3511, b;
b = a | 0xff;
printf("%d", b);
```

Ans. *0xff* is a hexadecimal number and hence will have 16 bits. Since there is a bitwise OR operation, we have to perform OR(||) operation on each bit of the two numbers. Now,

```
      3511 = 0000 1101 1011 0111
(0xff) 255 = 0000 0000 1111 1111
             0000 1101 1111 1111      (3583 in decimal), (0xdff in hexadecimal)
```

Q.9. Is there any direct method of converting binary number to an octal number or hexadecimal number?

Ans. Yes, in case of converting the binary number into an octal number, make pairs of 3 bits:-

Let us convert $(10011100)_2$ to octal number:-

```
010   011   100
 2     3     4      = (234)_8
```

Similarly, in case of converting to a hexadecimal number, make pairs of 4 bits:-

Let us convert $(10011100)_2$ to hexadecimal number:-

1001   1100

  9   12   = $(0x9c)_{16}$

Q.10. What is the use of **%i**?

Ans. **%i** is treated in the same way as the format specifier *%d*. For example:

```
printf("%i", 5*5);
```

will print 25 on the output screen.

UNSOLVED PROBLEMS

Q.1. Divide 84 by 16 without using any of the arithmetic operators?

Q.2. 2's complement of a binary number is equal to 1's complement of that number plus one added to it. Find the 2's complement of:
54, 63, 12, 9

Q.3. Negative numbers are written as binary numbers in 2's complement form. Write the following negative numbers as binary numbers:
-23, -4, -17, -134

Q.4. Find the value of the variable k in the following expressions:

a)
```
int k = 2;
k = k>>2 && k<<1;
```

b)
```
int k = 20;
k = (( k<<2 ) >> 3 ) >>2;
```

c)
```
int k = 0x2fe;
k = 2 * ( ~k );
```

d)
```
int k = 4;
k = k *= k << 2;
```

Q.5. Let one binary number A and a binary number B (used as mask) are given. What operation will you perform so that:-
a) All the bits of A are converted to 1 at those places for which bit value is 1 in mask B.
b) All the bits of A are converted to 0 at those places for which bit value is 0 in mask B.
c) First four bits of A are copied to the resulting binary number C and the rest of the bits are inverted.

Q.6. Convert the following octal numbers to hexadecimal number system:-
0245, 023, 0712, 0317

Q.7. Convert the following hexadecimal number to octal number system:-
0xe4, 0x45f, 0xa12, 0x2eda

Q.8. Perform the following operation on the binary numbers:-

   a) 10011 * 101

   b) 110110 * 1101

   c) 1000 * 10

   d) 111 * 11

CHAPTER 4

DECISION MAKING

In daily life, we come across various situations where we have to make decision whether to do some work or not. In **C** also, we have to make decisions while writing programs. In this chapter, we will see how we can use conditions in our program.

if

The *if* block helps us to make decisions in our programs. In the parenthesis of *if*, the expression is checked for correctness. If the value within the parenthesis is non-zero, the statement(s) within the *if* block { } are executed. If the value within parentheses is 0, then no statements within the *if* block are executed.

Here is the structure of the *if* statement:-

```
if(condition)
{
    ....................;
    ..statements..;
    ....................;
}
```

Example:

```
int main()
{
    int i = 20;
    if(i > 10)
    {
        printf("Value of variable i is greater than 10");
    }
}
```

Result: Value of i is greater than 10.

i > 20 returns 1 as the condition is *true*. Thus, *if* now internally will be treated like this:-

```
if(1)
{
    printf("Value of variable i is greater than 10");
}
```

which means that the statement within the *if* block will be executed and hence the result.

Let us see some more examples on *if-*

Example:

```
int age = 19;
if(age < 18)
{
    printf("You are not eligible for voting in elections");
}
```

Result:

Since the value of variable *age* is greater than *19*, the condition *age < 18* returns 0 which means the *if* will be treated like this:-

```
if(0)
{
    printf("You are not eligible for voting in elections");
}
```

and hence, the statement within the *if* block will not be executed.

Example:

```
if(42 % 6)
    printf("Hello to all of you");
```

Result:

This time the expression *42 % 6* will leave 0 due to the modular division. Again the *if* statement will be treated like this:-

```
if(0)
    printf("Hello to all of you");
```

and hence, the statement below the *if* will not be executed.

Note

If there is a single statement to be executed by *if*, we may avoid using { }

Look at the following *if* statements:-

```
1. int i = 2;
   if(i)                    /* treated as if(2) */
         printf("Hello");

2. int i;
   if(i = 5)                /* treated as if(5) */
         printf("Bye");
```

In both cases, there will be a non-zero value left in the ( ) of *if*. In the second case, there should be a comparison operator(= =) instead of the assignment operator(=).

Note

A common mistake programmers do is that they place a semicolon (;) after the *if()* statement.

```
int a = 3;
if(a < 5); /* semi-colon used by mistake */
{
    printf("%d is less than 5", a);
    printf("\nGood bye for now");
}
```

Result: 3 is greater than 5
        Good bye for now

Explanation:

Since the condition in the *if* evaluates to false(0), nothing should be printed on the screen. But due to the above mistake, the *if* statement will be treated by the compiler like this:-

```
if(a < 5)
;
{
    printf("%d is less than 5", a);
    printf("\nGood bye for now");
}
```

A semicolon is a null statement and is treated as part of *if* above. Also, if there is no { just after the *if*, it reads only next line which is **;** here.

If-else

Sometimes we have to take two-way decisions where we want to check a condition for both *true* and *false*.

For example, if it is night, go to sleep otherwise get ready and go to work.

Such conditions can be solved in **C** with the help of *if-else* statement. The structure of *if-else* is as follows:-

```
if(condition)
{
    ........................;
    ...statements......;
    ........................;
}
else
{
    ........................;
    ...statements......;
    ........................;

}
```

Example:

```
int i = 10;
if(i > 5 && i < 10)
    printf("Value of i is smaller than 10 but greater than 5");
else
    printf("Value of i is not in the range from 6 to 9");
```

Result:

Value of i is not in the range from 6 to 9

Here since the value of *i* is 10, the expression *i>5 && i<10* evaluates to *false* and hence *else* part will be executed.

Note

In the above example, since both *if* and *else* are executing a single statement, we may avoid using their curly brackets { }.

Program# 9

To check whether a number entered by the user is even or odd.

```c
#include<stdio.h>

int main()
{
    int num;

    printf("Enter a number : ");
    scanf("%d", &num);

    if(num % 2 == 0)
        printf("%d is even", num);
    else
        printf("%d id odd", num);

    return 0;
}
```

Run this program.

Nested if

Nesting means one inside another. Thus, nesting of *if* means putting one or more *if* statements inside the block of another *if*. There are many situations when we need to check a condition that depends on some other condition. For example:-

We want to test a number whether it is divisible by both 2 and 3. This can be done in two ways:-

```c
1) if(n%2 == 0 && n%3 == 0)
        printf("Number is divisible by 2 and 3");

2) if(n%2 == 0)
        if(n%3 == 0)
                printf("Number is divisible by 2 and 3");
```

Nested if-else

We can use one *if-else* statement inside another *if-else* statement whenever necessary. Let us check a situation in which we need nesting of *if-else*.

Program# 10

To find if a candidate can stand for an election seat. The conditions for filling the nomination are:

1. His/her age should be greater than or equal to 25.
2. He/she must be a graduate.
3. He/she must be an Indian citizen.

```c
#include<stdio.h>

int main()
{
    int age;
    char graduate, citizen, gender;

    printf("Enter your age : ");
    scanf("%d", &age);

    printf("Enter 'g' for graduate, 'o' for other : ");
    getchar();          /* Remove \n character left in input buffer */
    scanf("%c", &graduate);

    printf("Enter 'i' for Indian citizen, 'n' for NRI : ");
    getchar();
    scanf("%c", &citizen);

    printf("Enter sex, 'm' for male or 'f' for female : ");
    getchar();
    scanf("%c", &gender);

    if(age >= 25)
    {
        if(graduate == 'g')
        {
            if(citizen == 'i')
            printf("\nOK, you are eligible for an election seat");
            else
            printf("\nOnly Indians are eligible for an election seat");
```

```
        }
        else
            printf("\nOnly graduates are eligible");
    }
    else
        printf("\nYou are underage for an election seat");

    return 0;
}
```

Run this program.

Explanation:

Here we used a new function *getchar()*. To understand this, first we will learn the concept of *input buffer*. An input buffer is a temporary area that holds the characters that we read from the keyboard.

The *scanf()* function when tries to read a character from the keyboard, it first reads the contents of the input buffer. If it finds any character, it returns back to the program without reading from the keyboard.

Hence, to clear out the input buffer so that the *scanf()* can read directly from the keyboard input, we used the function *getchar()*.

This mostly becomes necessary when we input character after an integer. For example, let we entered 27 for age and pressed the enter key. The program will read 27 which matches the integer *age* but leaves the enter key character (\n) in the buffer. We used getchar() to remove this extra enter character from input buffer.

else if

When we want to execute one condition, we use *if*. When we want to execute any one condition out of two, we use *if-else* but when we want to execute one condition out of many, we use the following structure:-

```
if(condition 1)
{
    .........
}
else if(condition 2)
{
    ..........
}
```

```
else if(condition 3)
{
}
. . . . . . . . .
else
{
    . . . . . . . . .
}
```

Let us understand it more clearly with an example:-

Program# 11

Print the division of a student who got marks out of 100.

```c
#include<stdio.h>

int main()
{
    int marks;

    printf("Enter student marks : ");
    scanf("%d", &marks);

    if(marks < 0 || marks > 100)
        printf("Invalid marks");
    else if( marks >=75)
        printf("Distinction");
    else if( marks >= 60)
        printf("First division");
    else if( marks >=45)
        printf("Second division");
    else if( marks >=34)
        printf("Third division");
    else
        printf("Fail");

    return 0;
}
```

Run this program.

One more example:

Program# 12

Calculate the total salary of employee based on the following conditions:-

1) If clerk, house rent allowance = 0
   If supervisor, house rent allowance = 8% of basic salary
   If manager, house rent allowance = 15% of basic salary

2) If clerk, travelling allowance = 2% of basic salary
   If supervisor, travelling allowance = 3% of basic salary
   If manager, travelling allowance = 5% of basic salary

3) If clerk, other allowance = 0
   If supervisor, other allowance = 2% of basic salary
   If manager, other allowance = 5% of basic salary

```c
#include<stdio.h>
#include<stdlib.h>

int main()
{
    float basic = 0, other = 0, ta = 0, hra = 0, total = 0;
    char post;

    printf("Enter the basic salary : ");
    scanf("%f", &basic);

    printf("Enter post: c for clerk, s for supervisor and m for manager : ");
    /* remove enter key left in input buffer after entering basic salary */
    getchar();
    scanf("%c", &post);

    if(post == 'c')
    {
        hra = 0;
        ta = 2 * basic / 100;
        other = 0;
    }
```

```
   else if(post == 's')
   {
      hra = 8 * basic / 100;
      ta = 3 * basic / 100;
      other = 2 * basic / 100;
   }
   else if(post == 'm')
   {
      hra = 15 * basic / 100;
      ta = 5 * basic / 100;
      other = 5 * basic / 100;
   }
   else
   {
      printf("Invalid post");
      exit(0);                    /* Terminate program */
   }

   total = basic + ta + hra + other;

   printf("\nTotal salary of the employee is : %0.2f", total);

   return 0;
}
```

Run this program.

switch-case

The *switch* statement allows us to check the value of an integer or a character variable. **It is not used to check conditions**. Actually, *switch* is meant for checking the value of integer values only, but since each character has an ASCII value which in turn is an integer, hence we can check the values of character variables as well.

The structure of a *switch* block is:-

```
switch(variable)
{
   case value1:
      ...statements...;
      break;
```

```
case value2:
    ...statements...;
    break;
case value3:
    ...statements...;
    break;
    .........
default:
    ...statements...;
}
```

Let us check out the use of *switch* with an example:

Program# 13

Demonstrating the use of switch statement

```
#include<stdio.h>

int main()
{
    int i = 5;

    switch(i)
    {
        case 1:                          /* i == 1 */
            printf("Value of i is 1");
            break;
        case 3:                          /* i == 3 */
            printf("Value of i is 3");
            break;
        case 5:                          /* i == 5 */
            printf("Value of i is 5");
            break;
        default:
            printf("I don't know the value of i");
    }

    return 0;
}
```

Run this program.

Explanation:

Why should we use *switch*?

To make a program more logical.

To check the values of a variable efficiently.

The *break* statement is used to exit the *switch* block when a value is checked for a variable.

Program# 14

Print the number of days in a month with the help of switch.

It is assumed that February has 28 days in that year.

```c
#include<stdio.h>

int main()
{
    int month;

    printf("Enter the month number (1-12) : ");
    scanf("%d", &month);

    switch(month)
    {
        case 1:
        case 3:
        case 5:
        case 7:
        case 8:
        case 10:
        case 12:
                printf("31 days");
                break;
        case 4:
        case 6:
        case 9:
        case 11:
                printf("30 days");
                break;
```

```
        case 2:
              printf("28 days");
              break;
        default:
              printf("Invalid month");
    }

    return 0;
}
```

Run this program.

What will happen if we don't use *break* in *switch*? Here is a sample *switch* without *break* and below is the result of that:-

```
int i = 4;
switch(i)
{
    case 1:
        printf("\nValue of i is 1");
    case 4:
        printf("\nValue of i is 4");
    case 7:
        printf("\nValue of i is 7");
    case 9:
        printf("\nValue of i is 9");
        break;
    case 10:
        printf("\nValue of i is 10");
    default:
        printf("\nI don't know the value of i");
}
```

Result:

    Value of i is 4
    Value of i is 7
    Value of i is 9

Switch matches *i* with 4 and does not find break statement after it, hence it executes all the remaining cases until it finds a break again.

Here is an example that shows how a *switch* can also be used with characters.

Program# 15

```c
#include<stdio.h>

int main()
{
    char letter;

    printf("Enter the first letter of a country : ");
    scanf("%c", &letter);

    switch(letter)
    {
        case 'i':
        case 'I':
                printf("\nIt may be India");
                break;
        case 'r':
        case 'R':
                printf("\nIt may be Russia");
                break;
        case 'u':
        case 'U':
                printf("\nIt may be USA");
                break;
        case 'c':
        case 'C':
                printf("\nIt may be China");
                break;
        default:
                printf("\nI don't know");
    }

    return 0;
}
```

Run this program.

Conditional operator (? :)

Conditional operator is used to check an expression for *true* or *false* value and takes some action according to the result. It is also called *ternary operator* as it takes three operands. It is generally written as:-

> expression? if_true : if_false;
>
> or
>
> result = expression ? if_true : if_false;

This operator can also be treated as the short form of *if-else*. Let us check an example:

Program# 16

Demonstrate the use of ternary operator.

```c
#include<stdio.h>

int main()
{
    int a, b;

    printf("Enter two numbers : ");
    scanf("%d %d", &a, &b);    /* Read two integers in a single scanf() */

    a > b ? printf("Bigger number is %d", a) : printf("Bigger number is %d", b);

    return 0;
}
```

Run this program and enter the input like this: 5 6

The line:-

```c
a > b ? printf("Bigger number is %d", a) : printf("Bigger number is %d", b);
```

can also be written like this:-

```c
result = a > b ? a : b;
```

```c
printf("Bigger number is %d", result);
```

We also have to declare the variable *result* where we declared variables *a* and *b*.
Here are some other examples of conditional operator:-

1)
```
int i = 6;
y = i > 5 && i < 10 ? 30 : 40;
```

Result: y = 30

2)
```
'a' <'A' ? printf("Good") : printf("Bad");
```

Result: Bad

This is because the ASCII value of *a* is 97 and the ASCII value of 'A' is 65.

3)
```
int a = 4, b = 6, c = 1, d = 9, e = -3, y;
y = (a == 4) ? b<1 ? c>5 ? d>8 ? (e/3 == -1) ? 20 : 30 : 40 : 50 : 60 : 70;
```

Result: y = 60

The steps for solving the above expression are as follows:

```
y = (a == 4) ? b<1 ? c>5 ? d>8 ? ((e/3 == -1) ? 20 : 30) : 40 : 50 : 60 : 70;
y = (a == 4) ? b<1 ? c>5 ? (d>8 ? 20 : 40) : 50 : 60 : 70;
y = (a == 4) ? b<1 ? (c>5 ? 20 : 50) : 60 : 70;
y = (a == 4) ? (b<1 ? 50 : 60) : 70;

y = (a == 4) ? 60 : 70;
y = 60;
```

4)
```
int a = 4, b = 6, c = 9;
y = a>3 ? b<5 : c>5;
```

Result: y = 0

The above expression is nothing but:-

```
y = a>3 ? 0 : 1
```

as *b* < 5 is *false* and *c* > 5 is *true*.

SOLVED PROBLEMS

Q.1. Why *switch* statement works with integer and character values and not with float values?

Ans. The *switch* statement works only with integer values but since each character has its corresponding ASCII value, which in turn is an integer value.

Q.2. How can we convert a lowercase character to an upper case character and vice-versa?

Ans. The ASCII value of a lower case character lies in the range *97–122* and the ASCII value of upper case characters lies in the range *65–91*. The difference of ASCII values between lower case character and an upper case character is 32. Hence, to convert a lowercase character to uppercase, simply subtract 32 from its ASCII value and to convert an upper case character to lowercase, add 32 to its ASCII value.

Example:

```
char ch;
printf("Enter a character : ");
scanf("%c", &ch);

if(ch >= 65 && ch <= 91)
        printf("Upper case character, lower case is %c", ch + 32);
else if(ch >= 97 && ch <= 122)
        printf("Lower case character, upper case is %c", ch + 32);
else if(ch >=48 && ch <= 57)
        printf("A numeric character");
else
        printf("A special character");
```

Q.3. What is the meaning of the term flag?

Ans. A *flag* is nothing but a variable that helps us to make some decision and tells us the status of a condition. Look at the following example that tries to find whether the entered number is even or odd:-

Example:

```
int num, flag;
printf("Enter a number : ");
```

```
scanf("%d", &num);

flag = 1;   /* Let the number in 'num' is even */
if(num % 2 != 0)
{
        /* change the value of flag to indicate the number is odd */
        flag = !flag;
}
if(flag)          /* flag will have value 0 or 1 */
        printf("%d is an even number", num);
else
        printf("%d is an odd number", num);
```

It is not necessary that we use the name *flag* for such a variable. We can use any name we like but the name *flag* identifies what type of variable it is.

Q.4. Is it necessary to give the *default* option in a switch block?

Ans. No, it is only given when we wish to give some choice if none of the values in the *cases* matches the expression in *switch*.

Q.5. What is a block?

Ans. The part of a program that is inside the curly brackets { } is called a block. For example:-

The block of function *main()* is:-

```
main()
{

}
```

The block of *if()* is:-
```
if(condition)
{

}
```

Q.6. What are local and global variables?

Ans. A variable that is declared within a block is called a local variable to that block whereas a variable that is declared outside a block is called global to that block. For example:-

```
int a = 5;                       /* Global to main() block */
int main()
{
    /* No local variable found, prints global variable, value is 5 */
    printf("%d\n", a);

    int a = 6;                   /* Local to main() */
    {
        int a = 7;               /* Local to this block */
        printf("%d", a);         /* Prints the local variable, value is 7 */
    }

    printf("%d\n", a);           /* Prints the local variable, value is 6 */
}
```

> **Note**
>
> A variable should not be declared twice in a common block. There is no problem in declaring the same variable in different blocks.

Q.7. Which one of the two: local or global has higher preference?

Ans. From the above example, it should be clear that local variables are given higher preference.

Q.8. When should we use conditional operator?

Ans. Conditional operator works as a short form of *if-else* statement to check values of a variable. It is up to the programmer, how much he/she feels comfortable with the conditional operator.

Q.9. Can we nest a *switch* statement with *if*?

Ans. Yes, here is an example:-

```
int a = 5, b = 6;
if(a > 4)
{
    switch(b % 2 == 0)
    {
        case 0:
            printf("%d is greater than 4 and %d is even", a, b);
            break;
```

```
        case 1:
                printf("%d is greater than 4 and %d is odd", a, b);
                break;
        }
    }
```

Q.10. What is the meaning of the following statements:-

```
int a = 4;
if(a)
        printf("The value of a is non-zero");
else
        printf("The value of a is zero");
```

Ans. *if()* works only when there is non-zero value left in the (). In the above approach, we are trying to check whether the variable *a* is 0 or non-zero. If the value of *a* is non-zero, then *if()* will be executed and if the value of *a* is 0, then *else* will be executed.

UNSOLVED PROBLEMS

Q.1. What do you mean by the preference of a variable? Give example.

Q.2. Give the drawback of conditional operator.

Q.3. Where we can and cannot use *switch* statement?

Q.4. Give an example to differentiate between local and global scope of variables.

Q.5. What do you mean by nesting of if? Give example.

Q.6. Give results of the following expressions:-

```
a.  25 > 24 ? printf("Greater") : printf("Lesser");
b.  int a = 42 % 6 > 23 % 2 ? 1 : 0;
c.  printf("Good") > printf("Bad") ? printf("Smart") : printf("Idiot");
d.  int a = 0x2f;

      a << 4 < ~1 ? printf("Left shift") : printf("1's complement");
```

Q.7. Write a program to find the percentage of a student according to the sum of numbers obtained by him/her in each subject. The maximum marks for each subject is 100.

Q.8. Write a program to find whether the year entered by a user is a leap year or not.

Q.9. Write a program to print the ASCII value of any character entered by the user.

Q.10. Is there a way such that *if()* works when condition is false and *else* works when the condition is true?

Introduction to loops

Looping means doing a work again and again. In our programs, we may want to repeat a set of instructions many times like entering many numbers or printing a series of numbers. We can do this either by typing a set of statements many times in our program, or we can do this by using a looping structure provided by **C** which can automatically repeat the set of statements as many times as it is needed.

Following are the looping mechanisms that we can use in **C**:-

while loop

The *while* loop is the most basic of the looping structures in **C**. The structure of this loop is:-

```
while(condition)
{
    .............................;
    .......statements........;
    .............................;
}
```

The *while* loop checks whether there is any non-zero value in its ( ) or not. If there is a non-zero value, the statement within the *while* loop will be executed and if there is a 0, then the execution of the loop will be terminated and the program control will be transferred to the next line that comes after the *while* block.

The execution of the statements within the *while* loop is done like this:-

1. First the condition within ( ) of while is checked for a non-zero value.

2. If there is a non-zero value, the statements within the block { } will be executed, otherwise the program control will be transferred after the end of the while loop.

3. After executing the statements within the loop, the program control transfers at the beginning of the loop and the condition is checked again. This process continues until there is a 0 in the ( ) of while.

Here is a program that will print the square of first 10 natural numbers.

Program# 17

Print squares of first 10 numbers

```c
#include<stdio.h>

int main()
{
    int i = 1;                          /* start counting from 1 to 10 */

    /* loop continues till the value of 'i' is less than or equal to 10 */
    while(i <= 10)
    {
        printf("%d\t", i * i);          /* print square of 'i' */
        i = i + 1;                      /* increase value of 'i' */
    }

    return 0;
}
```

Run this program.

Result: 1   4   9   16   25   36   49   64   81   100

Explanation:

When the loop executes for the first time, the condition *1<=10* will be checked which returns 1 as 1 is less than 10. Then the square of 1 is printed and the value of the variable *i* is incremented by 1. Now the value of *i* is 2.

Again the condition in ( ) will be checked. This time *2<=10* is checked which will again return 1 as the condition is *true*. Again square of 2 is printed and the value of *i* is incremented by 1. This process continues until the value of *i* becomes 11. This time *11<=10* returns 0 as the condition is *false* and the program control will be transferred to the *return* line.

Let us write one more program.

Program# 18

Print all the even numbers from 30 to 10

Logic: First we have to move from 30 to 10 in the loop. For this we will take a loop counting variable *i* and set its initial value to 30. Then on every iteration, we will decrease the value of *i* by one.

To check whether the number is even, we will check if the value of *i* is divisible by 2 by using the % operator which returns the remainder. If the value of *i* is divisible by 2, the remainder will be 0.

```c
#include<stdio.h>

int main()
{
    int i = 30;                    /* start counting from 30 to 10 */

    /* loop continues till the value of i is greater than 0 */
    while(i > 0)
    {
        if(i % 2 == 0)             /* check if i is divisible by 2 */
            printf("%d   ", i);
        i = i - 1;                 /* decrease i by 1 */
    }

    return 0;
}
```

Run this program.

Result: 30   28   26   24   22   20   18   16   14   12   10

Conditional less while - break

It is possible to stop the execution of the *while* loop without giving any condition in its (). This can be done with the help of the keyword *break* within the body of the while loop. Here is an example that will show the use of *break* to stop the execution of the loop:-

Program# 19

Show the squares of first 10 numbers

```c
#include<stdio.h>

int main()
{
    int i = 1;     /* start counting from 1 to 10 */

    /* 1 is considered true, the loop will always execute */
    while(1)
    {
        printf("%d\t", i * i);
        i = i + 1;

        /* if value of i is greater than 10, stop execution of loop */
        if( i > 10)
            break;
    }

    return 0;
}
```

Run this program.

Result: 1   4   9   16   25   36   49   64   81   100

Program# 20

Print sum of numbers entered by the user

Logic: To repeatedly input numbers, we will put the *scanf()* statement in the loop. Each number entered by the user will be stored in a variable say *n* and its value will be added to another variable *sum* that stores the sum of all the numbers entered by the user.

Finally, we will print this sum after the end of the execution of the loop.

```c
#include<stdio.h>

int main()
{
    int i, n, val, sum;

    printf("How many numbers you want to enter ? ");
    scanf("%d", &n);

    i = 1;
    sum = 0;        /* Initialize sum to 0 for the first time */
    while(i <= n)
    {
        printf("Enter the number : ");
        scanf("%d", &val);

        /* add val to old value of sum and store in sum */
        sum = sum + val;
        i = i + 1;
    }

    printf("The sum of numbers you entered is : %d", sum);

    return 0;
}
```

Run this program.

Looping on demand

In the above program, we asked the user how many numbers he/she wants to enter. But it is also possible to ask the user whether the user wants to enter more numbers or not.

Here is a program that will show how we can do this:-

Program# 21

Find the sum of numbers entered by the user. This time if the user wants to stop entering number in the middle, he/she can do so.

```c
#include<stdio.h>

int main()
{
    int val, sum;
    char choice;

    sum = 0;
    while(1)                      /* No condition */
    {
        printf("Do you want to enter number (y/n)? ");
        choice = getchar();        /* Read one character */

        if( choice != 'y')
              break;

        printf("\nEnter number:");
        scanf("%d", &val);

        /* remove enter key pressed after number */
        getchar();

        sum = sum + val;
    }

    printf("\n\nThe sum of numbers you entered is %d", sum);

    return 0;
}
```

Run this program.

Skipping statements of a loop - continue

Sometimes we need to skip some statements within the loop based on some condition. For example, we are given a problem in which we have to print the squares of all numbers that are not divisible by 3. For this, we can use the keyword *continue* which transfers the program control back to the condition checking.

Here is an example program:-

Program# 22

Print squares of all numbers up to 10 that are not divisible by 3

```c
#include<stdio.h>

int main()
{
  int i;

  i = 0;
  while(i < 10)
  {
    i = i + 1;

    /* skip remaining statements of while loop if i is divisible by 3 */
    if(i % 3 == 0)
        continue;

    printf("%d ", i * i);
  }

  return 0;
}
```

Run this program.

Result: 1   4   16   25   49   64   100

Comparison - break & continue

break and *continue* are **C** keywords that work with a loop. *break* is used to stop the execution of the loop whereas *continue* is used to skip remaining statements of the loop but continue the execution of the loop.

Here is a comparison between the two:-

```c
int a = 0;              int a = 0;
while(a < 20)           while(a < 20)
{                       {
    a++;                    a++;
    if(a % 5 == 0)          if(a % 5 == 0)
```

```
    break;                      continue;
    printf("%d ", a);           printf("%d ", a);
}                           }
```

Result: 1 2 3 4   1 2 3 4 6 7 8 9 11 12 13 14 16 17 18 19

A common mistake

A common mistake we do while using a loop is that we place a semicolon (;) after the *()* of the while loop. For example:

```
int a = 5;
while(a < 10);
{
    printf("\n%d", a);
    a++;
}
```

Result:

The above loop will not stop executing and is hence an infinite loop. This is because ; is a null statement due to which *while* loop will be forced to execute only a single line which is ;. The statements within the block *{ }* will not be treated as the part of the while loop.

Nested while

Nesting of while means using one while loop within another while loop. Let us look at the following situation where we want to print the factorial of a number. So, we can write a loop like this:

```
i = 1;
f = 1;
while(i <= n)
{
    f = f * i;
    i++;
}

printf("%d", f);
```

Here *n* is any number whose factorial we want to calculate. Now someone told us that we have to print the factorials of first 5 natural numbers. For this, we will use another loop that will count the numbers from 1 to 5. Thus, we can write a program for the above problem like this:-

Program# 23

Print the factorials of first 5 natural numbers

Logic: We will use one loop that will count from 1 to 5. Then we will use another nested loop that will calculate the factorial of the counter variable.

```c
#include<stdio.h>

int main()
{
    int i, j;
    long f;

    printf("Printing factorial of first 5 natural numbers\n\n");

    i = 1;

    /* This loop counts from 1 to 5 */
    while(i <= 5)
    {
        f = 1;
        j = 1;

        /* Calculate factorial of value of i */
        while(j <= i)
        {
            f = f * j;
            j++;
        }

        printf("\nFactorial of %d is %ld", i, f);
        i++;
    }

    return 0;
}
```

Run this program.

Result: Factorial of 1 is 1

Factorial of 2 is 2

Factorial of 3 is 6
Factorial of 4 is 24
Factorial of 5 is 120

do-while loop

This is also a looping structure that is commonly used. It works exactly like *while* but with one slight difference.

A while loop checks the condition first and then executes the statement within its block. If the condition is *false* for the very first time, the loop will not execute any of the statements within its block.

On the other hand, the *do-while* loop checks the condition at the end of the loop block. This means the *do-while* loop will be executed at least once even if the condition is *false* for the first time.

Here is the structure of a *do-while* loop:-

```
do
{
    ...................;
    ..statements..;
    ...................;
}while(condition);
```

Program# 24

```c
#include<stdio.h>

int main()
{
    int bill;
    int option;
    char choice;

    do
    {
        printf("\n1. Burger - 60");
        printf("\n2. Sandwich - 80");
        printf("\n3. Pasta - 100");
        printf("\n4. Spaghetti - 150");
```

```c
printf("\n\nDo you want to order something (y/n) ? ");
choice = getchar();

if(choice == 'y')
{
        printf("\nEnter option 1-4: ");
        scanf("%d", &option);
        getchar();

        switch(option)
        {
                case 1:
                        bill += 60;
                        break;
                case 2:
                        bill += 80;
                        break;
                case 3:
                        bill += 100;
                        break;
                case 4:
                        bill += 150;
                        break;
                default:
                        printf("\nInvalid option selected");
                        break;
        }
}
else if(choice == 'n')
{
        printf("\nOk fine");
}
else
{
        printf("\nInvalid choice");
}
}while(choice == 'y');
```

```
if(bill > 0)
    printf("\n\nYour total bill = %d", bill);
else
    printf("\n\nWe hope you give us chance next time");

return 0;
}
```

Run this program.

Comparison - while & do-while

Here is the comparison between the two loops:-

Example:

```
int a = 5;                      int a = 5;
do                              while(a > 5 && a < 10)
{                               {
    printf("%d ", a);               printf("%d ", a);
    a++;                            a++;
}while(a > 5 && a < 10);        }
```

Result: 5 6 7 8 9   No result.

while loop never executes as the condition is *false* for the very first time.

for loop

for() loop is another looping structure with some extra features than *while*. The structure of *for* loop is as follows:-

```
for(expression 1 ; condition ; expression 2)
{
    ....................;
    ...statements...;
}
```

expression 1 will be executed for the first time and only once. This can be used to give initial values to the loop counter. The *condition* part specifies how long the *for* loop will be executed. This is same as the condition part of the *while* loop. The *expression 2* part will be executed after executing the loop body. Hence, we can also write the structure of the *for* loop like this:-

```
for(initialize counter ; condition ; increment/decrement counter)
{
    ......................;
    ...statements...;
}
```

An example of a *for* loop that prints the squares of numbers from 1 to 10 is as follows:-

Example:

```
int i;
for(i = 1; i <= 10; i++)
{
    printf("%d ", i);
}
```

Result: 1   4   9   16   25   36   49   64   81   100

Explanation:

First the value of the loop counter *i* is initialized to 1 and is done only once. Then, the condition is checked. After this, the value of *i* is printed. Then the value of *i* is incremented by 1 by the statement *i++*. The *for* loop is very flexible and can also be written in the following ways:-

```
1) for(i = 1; i <= 10; printf("%d ", i), i++)
   ;

2) for(i = 1; i <= 10; printf("%d ", i), i++)
   { }

3) for(;;)           /* All the three parts are left empty */
   {
        if(i > 10)
            break;

        printf("%d ", i);
            i++;
   }
```

Cleary, we can see that none of the parts of a *for* loop are compulsory.

Developing logic

Programming does not involve only running the program and getting the desired result. The most important part is creating *logic* for the program. If the concepts of a programmer are clear, s/he can learn any programming language very easily and can write complex programs efficiently.

Here are some examples in which we will first try to figure out the logic and then write the programs:-

1. Find the factorial of a number.

Logic. Let the number whose factorial we want to calculate is 5 i.e. n = 5.

Now, 5! = 1 x 2 x 3 x 4 x 5   which is equal to 120.

We will solve it step by step as:-

```
 1 x 1 = 1
 1 x 2 = 2
 2 x 3 = 6
 6 x 4 = 24
24 x 5 = 120
```

Clearly, we need a loop that iterates 5 times i.e. *n* times.

```
for(i = 1; i <= n; i++)
{

}
```

Now, the right side of multiplication is increasing - 1 2 3 4 5, etc. In our loop, the value of the variable *i* is also increasing in the same order.

```
for(i = 1; i <= n; i++)
{
    x i                 /* Something like this to be done */
}
```

Now, the result of multiplication has to be stored in some variable. Hence, the loop now looks like:-

```
for(i = 1; i <= n; i++)
{
    f = ? x i;       /* Let f stores the result at each step */
}
```

From the step by step multiplication we have written, we can clearly see that the result that was stored in the variable *f* is multiplied by *i* on the next line. Hence, the loop now is:-

```
for(i = 1; i <= n; i++)
{
    f = f x i;
}
```

Also, first time we multiplied *1 x 1*, hence the first value of *f* should be 1. Hence, the loop for factorial becomes:-

```
for(i = 1, f = 1; i <= n; i++)
{
    f = f x i;
}
```

Now, a complete program to find the factorial of a number can be written like this:-

Program# 25

Print factorial of a number.

```
#include<stdio.h>

int main()
{
    int i, n;
    long f;          /* Factorial can be a big value */

    printf("Enter the number : ");
    scanf("%d", &n);

    for(i = 1, f = 1; i <= n; i++)
        f = f * i;

    printf("The factorial of %d is %ld", n, f);

    return 0;
}
```

Run this program.

2. To find the power of a number

Logic. The logic for this is very much similar to the logic of factorial.

Let we want to raise 3 to the power 5 i.e. 3^5 (n^p)

Now, $3^5 = 3 \times 3 \times 3 \times 3 \times 3$

We will write this again step by step like this:-

```
1 x 3 = 3
3 x 3 = 9
9 x 3 = 27
27 x 3 = 81
81 x 3 = 243
```

The above multiplication is repeated 5 times, i.e. as many times as the power of the number. Hence, we can write a loop that will loop up to the value of *p* like this:-

```
for(i = 1; i <= p; i++)
{

}
```

Now again, 3 i.e. n is multiplied at each step. Also, the result need to be stored in some variable say *x*. Again the value of *x* is multiplied by *n* at next step, hence, the loop can be written as:-

```
x = 1;                      /* First value of x */
for(i = 1; i <= p; i++)
{
    x = x * n;         /* n multiplied at each step */
}
```

Now, the complete program to find the power of a number can be written as:-

Program# 26

Calculate the power of a number

```
#include<stdio.h>

int main()
{
    int i, n, p;
    long x;                     /* Power can be a big value */

    printf("Enter the number : ");
    scanf("%d", &n);
```

```
printf("Enter the power : ");
scanf("%d", &p);

x = 1;                          /* First value of x */
for(i = 1; i <= p; i++)
    x = x * n;

printf("%d raise to the power %d is %ld", n, p, x);

return 0;
}
```

Run this program.

3. To reverse the digit of numbers

Logic. Let us take a number *12345* which is to be reversed.

We will write the reversing of this number step by step like this:-

    5
    54
    543
    5432
    54321

Now, the above can be written as:-

5	5	where	12345 % 10 = 5
54	5 x 10 + 4		1234 % 10 = 4
543	54 x 10 + 3		123 % 10 = 3
5432	543 x 10 + 2		12 % 10 = 2
54321	5432 x 10 + 1		1 % 10 = 1

Clearly, we have to take the remainder at each step. We also multiply each time the previous value by 10 and add the remainder to it. Also, we have to remove the last digit of the remaining number which can be done by dividing the number by 10 as integer don't accept digits after decimal.

Here is the program for above discussion:-

Program# 27

Print the reverse of a number

```c
#include<stdio.h>

int main()
{
    long sum = 0, n;

    printf("Enter the number : ");
    scanf("%ld", &n);

    /* Loop till the value of 'n' is non-zero */
    while(n)
    {
        sum = sum * 10 + n % 10;
        n = n / 10;
    }

    printf("The reversed number is %ld", sum);

    return 0;
}
```

Run this program.

4. To calculate the sum of the following series:-

$1 + 3/2! + 5/3! + 7/4!$ ....

Logic: In this problem, we need two loops. One loop will count from 1 to n i.e. the number of terms whereas other loop is required to calculate the factorial of the denominator. If i be the loop counter that loops from 1 to n, then we write the problem as:-

i = 1		i = 2		i = 3		i = 4	
1	+	3/2!	+	5/3!	+	7/4!	....

The numerator can be calculated with the formula:- $2 * i - 1$

The denominator is the factorial of the value of i

Here is the program:-

Program# 28

Print the sum of the following series:-

1 + 3/2! + 5/3! + 7/4! ....

```c
#include<stdio.h>

int main()
{
    int i, j, n, f;
    float sum;

    printf("Enter the number of terms in the series : ");
    scanf("%d", &n);

    sum = 0;

    for(i = 1; i <= n; i++)
    {
        f = 1;
        for (j = 1; j <= i; j++)              /* Factorial of i */
            f = f * j;

        sum = sum + (float)(2 * i - 1) / f;
    }

    printf("The sum of the series %f", sum);

    return 0;
}
```

Run this program.

5. Print the following series:-

```
   *
  * *
 * * *
* * * *
 * * *
  * *
   *
```

i.e. if the user enters 4 as the length of the series.

Logic: We will break the above figure in two parts as:-

```
   *
  * *
 * * *
* * * *
```

and

```
* * *
 * *
  *
```

To print the upper part, first, we require a loop that will count from 1 to n. Here the value of n is 4. Then we require a loop that will print blank spaces to make the figure in triangle form. At last, we need a loop to print the repetitive *.

The upper part now can be written as:-

```
i = 1        *
i = 2       * *
i = 3      * * *
i = 4     * * * *
```

The number of * printed on each line is equal to the value of the loop counter *i*. Hence, we will use a loop that will count from 1 to *i* to print the '*'.

To print the lower part, first we require a loop that will count from 1 to n – 1 (one less). Then we require a loop that will print blank spaces to make the figure in triangle form. At last, we need a loop to print the repetitive *.

The lower part now can be written as:-

```
* * *   i = 1   * printed = 4 - 1 i.e. n - 1
 * *    i = 2   * printed = 4 - 2 i.e. n - 2
  *     i = 3   * printed = 4 - 3 i.e. n - 3
```

Here is the complete program to print the above discussed figure:-

Program# 29

Print the following series:-

```
        *
       * *
      * * *
     * * * *
      * * *
       * *
        *
```

```c
#include<stdio.h>

int main()
{
    int i, j, n;

    printf("Enter the length of the series : ");
    scanf("%d", &n);

    for(i = 1; i <= n; i++)                      /* Upper part */
    {
        for(j = 1; j <= 20 - i; j++)        /* Print spaces */
                printf(" ");

        for(j = 1; j <= i; j++)             /* Print '*' */
                printf("* ");

        printf("\n");                       /* Move to the next line */
    }

    for(i = 1; i <= n - 1; i++)                  /* Lower part */
    {
        /* 20-n+i  because space is increasing */

        for(j = 1; j <= 20 - n + i; j++)
                printf(" ");
```

```
        for(j = 1; j <= n - i; j++)
                printf("* ");

        printf("\n");
    }

    return 0;
}
```

Run this program.

Explanation:

The upper part will print *20 - n* number of spaces on the last step. Hence, in the lower part, the number of spaces to be print will be *20 - n + 1*.

goto

goto transfers the control of the program to any marked line or label in the program. The use of *goto* is not considered good in **C** by many programmers because it complicates the flow of the program. Also, it is very difficult to trace the sequence of execution of program statements that has many *goto* statements. Here is an example that will show how we can use *goto* in our program:-

Program# 30

Force user to input only even number

```
#include<stdio.h>

int main()
{
    int n;

again:
    printf("\nEnter an even number : ");
    scanf("%d", &n);

    if(n % 2 != 0)
    {
        printf("The number is not even, please enter again...\n");
        goto again;
    }
```

```
    printf("You entered an even number");

    return 0;
}
```

Run this program.

Explanation:

In the above program, *again* is any name given to the statement. The line:-

goto again;

transfers the control back to the part of the program that is given the name *again*. It then moves to the *printf()* function that prompts the user to again enter the number.

Let us use *goto* statement that will provide a looping structure. It calculates the sum of any *n* numbers entered by the user.

Program# 31

Find sum of numbers entered by the user by using the goto statement

```
#include<stdio.h>

int main()
{
    int val, sum = 0;
    char ch;
again:
    printf("\nDo you want to enter number y/n? : ");
    ch = getchar();

    if(ch != 'y')
        goto end;

    printf("\nEnter number : ");
    scanf("%d", &val);

    getchar();

    sum = sum + val;

    goto again;
```

```
        end:

        printf("\nThe sum of numbers is %d", sum);

        return 0;
}
```

Run this program.

The same logic can be developed efficiently by using *do-while* loop like this:

Program# 32

Find sum of numbers entered by the user using do-while loop

```
#include<stdio.h>

int main()
{
    int val, sum = 0;
    char ch;

    do
    {
        printf("\nDo you want to enter number y/n ? : ");
        ch = getchar();

        if(ch != 'y')
            break;

        printf("\nEnter number : ");
        scanf("%d", &val);
        getchar();        /* remove \n character from input buffer */

        sum = sum + val;
    }while(ch == 'y');

    printf("\nThe sum of numbers is %d", sum);

    return 0;
}
```

Run this program.

SOLVED PROBLEMS

Q.1. What is a counter in a loop?

Ans. A counter is a variable that is used to count the number of times the loop is executed.

Example:

```
for (i = 1; i <= 10; i++)
      printf("\n%d", i);
```

Here the variable *i* is acting as the loop counter.

Q.2. What is an infinite loop?

Ans. A loop that has no stopping/ending is called an infinite loop.

Example:

```
for (; ;)                   for(; 20 ;)
{                           {
      ..statements..              ..statements..
}                           }
      while(1)                    do
{                           {
      ..statements..              ..statements..
}                           }while(5);
```

Q.3. Can a *for()* loop be nested with a *while()* or a *do-while()* loop?

Ans. Yes, take a look at the following example:-

Example:

```
for (i = 1; i <= 3; i++)
{
      j = 1;
      while(j <= 3)
      {
            printf("%d \t %d", i, j);
            j++;
      }
```

```
        printf("\n");
}
```

Result: 11   12   13
                21   22   23
                31   32   33

Q.4. What is the difference between *break* and *continue* statements?

Ans. The purpose of the *break* statement is to stop the execution of the loop whereas *continue* statement is used to skip the rest of the lines of the loop and transfers the control to the first line of the loop.

Q.5. What is the difference between *conditional* and *unconditional goto* statements?

Ans. *Unconditional goto* simply transfers the control from one part of the program to other part whereas *conditional goto* transfers the control from one part of the program to other on some specified condition.

Q.6. Can we use goto statement for looping?

Ans. Yes, look at the following program segment:-

Example:

```
        int i = 1, f = 1;
again:
        f = f * i;
        i++;
        if(i <= 5)
                goto again;

        printf("\nFactorial of %d is %d", 5, f);
```

Q.7. Give the output:-

```
int a, b = 5;
a = b++ * b-- - 4 * ++b / 3 - --b + ++b;
printf("%d  %d", a, b);
```

Ans. Following are the steps to solve above problem:-

1. a = b++ * b-- - 4 * ++b/3 - --b + ++b;
       5   5   5   5   5

2. a = b++ * b-- - 4 * b/3 - --b + ++b;
       6   6   6   6   6   `/* because of first ++b */`

3. a = b++ * b-- - 4 * b/3 - b + ++b;
       6   6   6   6   6   `/* because of --b */`

4. a = b++ * b-- - 4 * b/3 - b + b;
       6   6   6   6 6   `/* because of ++b */`

5. a = b * b - 4 * b/3 - b + b;
       6 6   6   6 6   `/* b++ and b-- are not solved on this line */`

6. a = 6 * 6 - 4 * 6/3 - 6 + 6;
   a = 36 - 24/3
   a = 28

Now, *b++* and *b--* will be solved. The value of *b* is increased first by 1 and then decreased by 1, hence no change.

Result: 28   6

Q.8. Can a *while()* loop have a comma (,) in its ()?

Ans. Yes, we can place a comma in the condition part of the *while* loop. Look at the following example:-

Example:

```c
#include<stdio.h>

int main()
{
    char ch;
    while((printf("Press any key : "), ch = getch()) != 'q')
            printf("%d\n", ch);

    return 0;
}
```

SOLVED PROGRAMS

Q.1. To print the following series:-

```
A B C D E D C B A
A B C D   D C B A
A B C       C B A
A B           B A
A               A
```

Logic: First we will write the following things about the above series:

1. We can print the characters with the help of *printf("%c", value)*
2. We will need a main loop that will count the series from top to bottom.
3. Then we will need another loop that will print the increasing series 'A B C D.'
4. A loop is required that will print the spaces between the increasing and decreasing series.
5. Another loop is required that will print the decreasing series '..D C B A'

```c
#include<stdio.h>

int main()
{
    int n, i, j;

    printf("Enter the limit:");
    scanf("%d", &n);

    printf("The series is\n\n");
    for(i = 1; i <= n; i++)

    {

        /*This loop will print the increasing part*/
        for(j = 1; j <= n - i; j++)
            printf("%c ", j + 64);

        /*This loop will print the spaces*/
        for(j = 1; j <= 4 * (i - 2) + 2; j++)
            printf(" ");
```

```
        /* This loop will print the decreasing part */
        for(j = n - i; j >= 1; j--)
        {
                /* skip first character on first line */
                if(i == 1 && j == n - i)
                        continue;
                printf("%c ", j + 64);
        }

        printf("\n");

    }

    return 0;
}
```

Run this program.

Explanation:

If you note in the series, the decreasing part has 'D C B A' twice if you entered the limit 5. Thus, we have to stop printing *E* for the first time in the decreasing part. That is why we used the *if()* as:-

```
if(i == 1 && j == n - i)
        continue;
```

i.e. do nothing when the loop is executed for the first time.

Q.2. Print the following series:-

```
        1
      2   2
    3   3   3
  4   4   4   4
  ----------------
```

Logic: To print the above series, we will divide it into three parts:-

  a. First the series is moving in a downward direction.
  b. Second there are spaces printed on the left side to make the figure look triangular
  c. Third the values are printed.

We will use a loop to count the number of lines first. Let this is done by the loop counter *i*. Now we write the series as:

1	i = 1
2 2	i = 2
3 3 3	i = 3
4 4 4 4	i = 4

Clearly, the value of *i* is printed on each line. A loop is required to print the values. Another loop is required to print the spaces on the left side.

```c
#include<stdio.h>

int main()
{
    int i, j, n;

    printf("Enter the limit : ");
    scanf("%d", &n);

    /* This loop will count the number of lines to be printed */
    for(i = 1; i <= n; i++)
    {
        /* This loop will print the spaces */
        /* Let 20 spaces printed for first time */
        for(j = 1; j <= 20 - i; j++)
            printf(" ");

        for(j = 1; j <= i; j++)
            printf("%d ", j);

        printf("\n");
    }

    return 0;
}
```

Q.3. To print prime numbers up to a given number.

Logic: A prime number is that number which is divisible by 1 or itself.

Let the number be *n*. We will try to divide *n* from 2 to *n/2*. If it is divisible by any number in this range, then it is not a prime number otherwise it is a prime number.

```c
#include<stdio.h>

int main()
{
    int i, j, n, prime;

    printf("Primes upto what number ? ");
    scanf("%d", &n);

    printf("\nPrinting prime numbers now...\n\n");

    for(i = 1; i <= n; i++)
    {
        prime = 1;  /* Let the value of 'i' is prime */
        for(j = 2; j <= i / 2; j++)
            if(i % j == 0)
            {
                prime = 0;       /* Value of 'i' is not prime */
                break;
            }

        if(prime == 1)                  /* or we may write if(prime) */
            printf("%d\n", i);

    }

    return 0;
}
```

Q.4. To check whether a number is Armstrong or not.

Logic: An Armstrong number is that whose sum of cubes of digits is equal to the number itself.

e.g. $371 = 3^3 + 7^3 + 1^3$

Let the number to be checked is n. We will use a loop that will move from 1 to n. We will check each value from 1 to n for Armstrong number.

```c
#include<stdio.h>

int main()
{
    int i, j, arm, sum, k;

    printf("Armstrong's up to what number ? ");
    scanf("%d", &arm);

    for(i = 1; i <= arm; i++)
    {
        sum = 0;
        j = i;
        while(j)
        {
            k = j % 10;
            sum += k * k * k;
            j /= 10;
        }

        if(sum == i)
            printf("\n%d is Armstrong", sum);

    }

    return 0;
}
```

Q.5. To print the Fibonacci series.

Logic: The Fibonacci series is:-

  0 1 1 2 3 5 8 13 21...

Let the first two terms of this series are 0 and 1. Rest each number is the sum of two previous numbers.

Let the first two terms are represented by a = 0, b = 1. Then next term will be $c = a + b$. After that, we change b to a by $a = b$ and c to b by b = c. Again, $c = a + b$ is calculated and so on.

```c
#include<stdio.h>

int main()
{
   int a, b, c, n, i;

   printf("How many numbers in the series ? ");
   scanf("%d", &n);

   a = 0,  b = 1;

   printf("\nThe series is...\n");
   for(i = 1; i <= n; i++)
   {
      if(i == 1)                      /* First term */
            printf("%d\t", a);
      else if(i == 2)                 /* Second term */
            printf("%d\t", b);
      else
      {
            c = a + b;
            printf("%d\t", c);
            a = b;
            b = c;
      }
   }

   return 0;
}
```

CHAPTER 6

Array basics

Normally in our programs, we need to declare and use variables. If we use a few numbers of variables, we may declare them by giving them names like a,b,c, etc. But what if we want to use 50 variables? We can't declare 50 variables as it would be tough and painful to remember them. That is when arrays come into the picture.

An array is a collection of similar type of elements. The elements in the array are used by the same name but different index number (position in the array). An array is declared by placing a [] after the array name.

For example, if we want to declare an array of 30 integers, we can write:

```
int ar[30];
```

The name of array in the above statement is *ar* which can be any user-defined name. The values in the array can be used like this:

```
ar[0]       first value
ar[1]       second value
ar[2]       third value
```

.

.

.

```
ar[29]      last value
```

The values in an array are always positioned (indexed) from 0 to size-1 where size is the number of elements in the array.

But why the array index starts with 0?

To find out, let us look at the following figure:

10	20	30	40	50	60	70	80

From the figure, we can see that we can get 20 by skipping 1 array element => ar[1], we can get 30 by skipping 2 array elements => ar[2] and we can get 10 by skipping 0 array elements => ar[0]. Hence, the array index starts at 0.

In terms of memory, we can write:

```
ar[1] = location of ar[0] + 2 bytes       (since the size of int is 2 bytes)
ar[2] = location of ar[0] + 4 bytes   or  location of ar[1] + 2 bytes
ar[3] = location of ar[0] + 6 bytes   or  location of ar[2] + 2 bytes
```

etc.

Initializing arrays

An array can be initialized with some default values. Here is an example:

```
int ar[5];               /* declare an array of 5 elements */

ar[0] = 10;              /* put values in each element one by one */
ar[1] = 20;
ar[2] = 30;
ar[3] = 40;
ar[4] = 50;
```

Obviously, this is a lengthy way of initializing an array. Here is a better way of doing this:

```
int ar[] = { 10, 20, 30, 40, 50 };
```

This will set *ar[0]* to 10, *ar[1]* to 20 and so on…

Reading arrays

We can read the values in the array efficiently using a loop. Here is an example:

```
int ar[] = { 10, 20, 30, 40, 50 };
int i;

for(i = 0; i < 5; i++)
    printf("%d  ", ar[i]);
```

When the loop starts, the value of *i* is 0, hence the *printf()* statement becomes:

```
printf("%d", ar[0]);        and the first value gets printed
```

When the value of *i* becomes *1, ar[1]* gets printed and so on…

Let us check out a program that demonstrates how we can initialize and print elements in the array.

Program# 33

Demonstrate initialization and printing of array elements.

```c
#include<stdio.h>

int main()
{
    int i;
    int ar[] = { 10, 20, 30, 40, 50 };

    for(i = 0; i < 5; i++)
        printf("%d  ", ar[i]);

    return 0;
}
```

Run this program.

> **Note**
>
> Some programmers write for loop like this:
>
> `for(i = 0; i <= 4; i++){`
>
> while others write:
>
> `for(i = 0; i < 5; i++){`
>
> Both are the same, it's up to you, which style you prefer. I will follow the second one.

Let us check out one more programs that finds the biggest number in the array.

Program# 34

Find the biggest number in the array.

```c
#include<stdio.h>

int main()
{
    int i, big;
    int ar[] = {50, 80, 30, 70, 40};

    /* assume that the first number is the biggest */
    big = ar[0];

    /* starting at position 1 as big is already ar[0] */
    for(i = 1; i < 5; i++)
    {
        if(big < ar[i])
                big = ar[i];
    }

    printf("The biggest number in the array is %d", big);

    return 0;
}
```

Run this program.

Explanation:

To find the biggest number in the array, we initialized the first number as the biggest number. Then we have compared our assumed biggest number with other numbers in the array. If we find an array element bigger than our assumed number, we mark that number as the biggest number. The loop continues to compare each number with the currently assumed biggest number and at the end; we get the biggest number in the array.

User input in arrays

We can ask a user to input values in the array instead of initializing array ourselves. Here is a program that asks the user to input values in the array and then calculates the sum of all entered numbers.

Program# 35

Ask a user to input numbers in the array and find the sum of all numbers.

```c
#include<stdio.h>

int main()
{
    int i, sum = 0;
    int ar[5];

    printf("Enter 5 numbers in the array : ");

    for(i = 0; i <= 4; i++)
        scanf("%d", &ar[i]);

    for(i = 0; i < 5; i++)
        sum = sum + ar[i];

    printf("The sum of numbers in the array is %d", sum);

    return 0;
}
```

Run this program.

Explanation:

The *scanf()* statement is used to take user input. Here, we have placed the *scanf()* statement inside the *for loop*. When the loop starts, the *scanf()* statement becomes:

```c
scanf("%d", &ar[0]);
```
and hence the first number entered by user goes to *ar[0]*

The loop continues and the numbers input by the user are placed in the array one by one.

Note

Since &ar[i] represents location of array element, we can also use *scanf* like this:

```c
scanf("%d", ar + i);
```

Linear searching

Now we will try to find the occurrence of a number in array using linear searching. In linear searching, we compare each value with value to be searched (called search key) one by one. Whenever a match is found, we print the position where the match was found.

Here is the program:

Program# 36

Implementing linear searching in the array.

```c
#include<stdio.h>

int main()
{
    int i, key, size;
    int match_count = 0;
    int ar[50];                    /* declare big enough array */

    printf("How many numbers you want to enter in the array ? ");
    scanf("%d", &size);

    printf("Enter %d numbers in the array : \n", size);
    for(i = 0; i < size; i++)
        scanf("%d", &ar[i]);

    printf("Enter number to search : ");
    scanf("%d", &key);

    for(i = 0; i < size; i++)
    {
        if(key == ar[i])
        {
            printf("%d found at position %d\n", key, i+1);
            ++match_count;
        }
    }
}
```

```
printf("%d match found", match_count);

return 0;
}
```

Run this program.

> **Note**
>
> We declared a big array in our program which is not a good idea. Later in the book, we will learn how to create dynamic memory for the array.

Binary searching

Binary searching is a fast technique for search an element in the array but the condition is the array should be sorted. In this searching, the key is compared with the middle element of the array. Three conditions can occur:

1. If there is a match, print the position and search is complete
2. If key is greater than the middle value, then we will search in the right half of the array
3. If key is smaller than the middle value, then we will search in the left half of the array

```
middle = (start + end)/2
```

Let we have the following array:

10	20	30	40	50	60	70	80	90	100

Let us suppose we need to find 20 (key). So on the first go, we will compare key with middle of array which is 50. We can see that 20 is less than 50, hence now we will find key in the left part of the array:

10	20	30	40

This time key will be compared with 20 and we find the match. So we are able to find the key in only two steps.

Here is a program that searches number using binary searching:

Program# 37

Implement binary searching in the array where values are in ascending order.

```c
#include<stdio.h>

int main()
{
    int i, key, start, end, middle, size;
    int ar[50];                 /* declare big enough array */

    int found = 0;

    printf("How many numbers to enter in array ? ");
    scanf("%d", &size);

    printf("Enter %d numbers in the array (ascending order)\n", size);
    for(i = 0; i < size; i++)
        scanf("%d", &ar[i]);

    printf("Enter number to search : ");
    scanf("%d", &key);

    start = 0;
    end = size-1;

    while(start <= end)
    {
        middle = (start + end)/2;    /* find middle value */

        if(key < ar[middle])
        {
            /* we need to search left part, move end */
            end = middle - 1;
        }
        else if(key > ar[middle])
        {
            /* we need to search right part, move start */
            start = middle + 1;
        }
        else
        {
```

```
            printf("%d found at position %d", key, middle + 1);
            found = 1;
            break;
        }
    }

    if(found == 0)
        printf("%d not found", key);

    return 0;
}
```

Run this program.

Bubble sort

Sorting is a technique in which we arrange elements of the array in ascending or descending order.

In bubble sorting, two adjacent elements are compared. If the first element is greater than the second element, then the two elements are swapped (interchanged) otherwise we compare the next two elements. This process is repeated until the array is sorted.

The steps for sorting the following numbers using bubble sort are:

12   34   4   54   45   2

Step 1:	Compare 1st and 2nd numbers 12 34 4 54 45 2	Result 12 34 4 54 45 2
Step 2:	Compare 2nd and 3rd numbers 12 34 4 54 45 2	Result 12 4 34 54 45 2
Step 3:	Compare 3rd and 4th numbers 12 4 34 54 45 2	Result 12 4 34 54 45 2
Step 4:	Compare 4th and 5th numbers 12 4 34 54 45 2	Result 12 4 34 45 54 2
Step 5:	Compare 5th and 6th numbers 12 4 34 45 54 2	Result 12 4 34 45 2 54

After first round of steps, we can see that the biggest number in the array bubbles up i.e. placed at the end of the array. If we repeat the above steps 4 more times, we get the sorted array.

Let us write a program to implement bubble sorting.

Program# 38

Implement bubble sorting in array.

```c
#include<stdio.h>

int main()
{
    int i , j, temp, size;
    int ar[50];                 /* declare big enough array */

    printf("How many numbers to enter in array ? ");
    scanf("%d", &size);

    printf("Enter %d numbers in the array\n", size);
    for(i = 0; i < size; i++)
        scanf("%d", &ar[i]);

    /* This loop is used for counting, no need to start it with 0 */
    /* If there are 5 numbers in the array, we need to repeat 4 times */
    /* this loop will repeat the sorting process */
    for(i = 1; i < size; i++)
    {
        for(j = 0; j < size-i; j++)
        {
            if(ar[j] > ar[j+1])
            {
                temp = ar[j];
                ar[j] = ar[j+1];
                ar[j+1] = temp;
            }
        }
    }
    printf("The sorted array is \n");
    for(i = 0; i < size; i++)
        printf("%d  ", ar[i]);

    return 0;
}
```

Run this program.

Selection sort

In this technique, the smallest number in the array is found and swapped with the first element. Then the second smallest number in the array is found and swapped with the second element of the array. The process continues until the whole array is sorted.

The sorting of following numbers can be done as follows:

12   34   4   54   45   2

Step 1: Initialize 1^{rst} element (12) as the smallest number. Compare 12 with each remaining number in the array. If an array element is found smaller than 12, then mark that element as the smaller number. Continue to find if any smaller number exist and at the end, swap the smallest found number with the 1^{rst} element. Hence, the array now is:

2   34   4   54   45   12

Step 2: Initialize 2nd element (34) as the smallest number and do as we did in step 1. The array now is:

2   4   34   54   45   12

By repeating the process, we will get a sorted array.

Let us create a program to implement bubble sorting.

Program# 39

Implement selection sorting in the array.

```c
#include<stdio.h>

int main()
{
    int i , j, temp, position, small, size;
    int ar[50];

    printf("How many numbers to enter in array ? ");
    scanf("%d", &size);

    printf("Enter %d numbers in the array\n", size);
    for(i = 0; i < size; i++)
        scanf("%d", &ar[i]);

    for(i = 0; i < size; i++)
```

```
    {
        small = ar[i];
        position = i;

        /* Now find small number in the rest of the array, so, j = i+1 */
        for(j = i + 1; j < size; j++)
        {
            if(small > ar[j])
            {
                small = ar[j];
                position = j;
            }
        }

        /* swap the smallest found number with number initially selected */
        temp = ar[i];
        ar[i] = small;
        ar[position] = temp;

    }

    printf("The sorted array is \n");
    for(i = 0; i < size; i++)
        printf("%d  ", ar[i]);

    return 0;
}
```

Run this program.

Insertion sort

In this technique, there is no swapping of numbers. Instead, the smallest found element is inserted in the appropriate position and to make room for this element, all the array elements are shifted to the right side.

We can apply the insertion sort on given numbers with the following steps:

12   34   4   54   45   2

Step 1: Initialize 2nd element (34) and check whether there is any bigger number to the left of 34. If yes, note the position of the bigger number. Now shift the numbers from big to the right side until you encounter 34 and at last, put 34 in the place of big. Here, there is no big number found to the left of 34, hence the array remains the same.

12   34   4   54   45   2

Step 2: Initialize 3rd element (4) and do as mentioned in step 1. Here 12 is the last big number found. Shift 12 and 34 to the right and place 4 in the place of 12. The array now is:

4   12   34   54   45   2

By repeating this process, we will get a sorted array.

Let us write a program to implement insertion sort technique.

Program# 40

Implement insertion sort on the array.

```c
#include<stdio.h>

int main()
{
   int i , j, position, size, number;
   int ar[50];

   printf("How many numbers to enter in array ? ");
   scanf("%d", &size);

   printf("Enter %d numbers in the array\n", size);
   for(i = 0; i < size; i++)
      scanf("%d", &ar[i]);

   for(i = 1; i < size; i++)
   {
      number = ar[i];
      position = i;

      /* now find smallest number on the left side */
      for(j = i - 1; j >= 0; j--)
      {
          /* find and note position of small number found */
          if(number < ar[j])
              position = j;              /* note position of big number */
          else
```

```
            break;
    }

    /* right shift array elements from pos to the position we started*/
    for(j = i; j > position; j--)
        ar[j] = ar[j-1];

    /* store the initialized number in appropriate position */
    ar[position] = number;
}

printf("The sorted array is \n");
for(i = 0; i < size; i++)
    printf("%d   ", ar[i]);

return 0;
}
```

Run this program.

2-D array

A two-dimensional array can be considered an **array of arrays**. People standing in multiple lines for railway tickets represent a 2-D array. A matrix in math is also an example of 2-D array. For example:

```
1    4    5    8
7    6    9    3
8    2    3    6
```

The above matrix is an example of 2-D array. We can say that above 2-D array is an array of three 1-D arrays where each 1-D array has 4 numbers or elements.

The number of columns (element count) for each 1-D array (or row) remains the same.

Declaring 2-D array

A 2-D array can be declared with the following statement:

```
int ar[3][2];           /*2-D array with 3 rows and 2 columns*/
```

The array elements will have following positions in the array:

```
ar[0][0]    ar[0][1]
ar[1][0]    ar[1][1]
ar[2][0]    ar[2][1]
```

The formula for finding the position of an array element is simple:

```
1    4    5    8
7    6    9    3
8    2    3    6
```

Let we need to find the position of 9, we can see that if we skip 1 row and 2 columns, we reach 9, hence the position is ar[1][2]

Similarly, if we need to find the position of 2, we skip 2 rows and 1 column. Thus, the position of 2 is ar[2][1]

To find the position of 5, we skip 0 rows and two columns, hence the position is ar[0][2]

Initializing 2-D array

A 2-D array can be initialized with the following statements:

```
int ar[2][3] = {
        { 1, 2, 3},
        { 4, 5, 6}
    };
```

The resultant array would be:

```
1    2    3
4    5    6
```

Let us write a program to initialize and print a 2-D array.

Program# 41

Initialize and print a 2-D array

```
#include<stdio.h>

int main()
{
    int i, j;

    /* initialize a 2-D array with 2 rows, 3 columns */

    int ar[2][3] = {
            { 1, 2, 3},
            { 4, 5, 6}
    };
```

```
    /* 2 rows starting with index 0, hence i < 2 */

    for(i = 0; i < 2; i++)
    {
        /* 3 columns starting with index 0, hence j < 3 */
        for(j = 0; j < 3; j++)
            printf("%d\t", ar[i][j]);

        printf("\n");
    }

    return 0;
}
```

Run this program.

Explanation:

Since we have to move in rows and columns, we require two loops. Outer loop is used to read rows one by one, whereas the inner loop is used to read columns of a particular row. In the statement:

```
printf("%d\t", ar[i][j]);
```

The value of i is fixed in the inner loop and j keeps changing. Hence, when the value of i is 0 for the first time, we read the array as:

```
ar[0][0]    ar[0][1]    ar[0][2]…   etc.
```

Then after the inner loop completes, the value of i is incremented and becomes 1. Hence, we read the following values:

```
ar[1][0]    ar[1][1]    ar[1][2]…   etc.
```

Use of 2-D array in matrix

A matrix is a 2-D representation of numbers. Let us write some programs to work on the matrix.

Program# 42

Representation of matrix

```c
#include<stdio.h>

int main()
{
    int i, j, row, col;
    int ar[10][10];                    /* declare big enough matrix */

    printf("How many rows ? ");
    scanf("%d", &row);

    printf("How many columns ? ");
    scanf("%d", &col);

    printf("Enter %d numbers now " , row*col);

    for(i = 0; i < row; i++)
    for(j = 0; j < col; j++)
        scanf("%d", &ar[i][j]);

    printf("\nThe matrix is \n");

    for(i = 0; i < row; i++)
    {
        for(j = 0; j < col; j++)
            printf("%d\t", ar[i][j]);

        printf("\n");
    }

    return 0;
}
```

Run this program.

Addition of two matrices

Addition of two matrices requires two different matrices with the same number of rows and columns. The addition can be done like this:

1	2		5	6		1+5	2+6		6	8
3	4	+	7	8	=	3+7	4+8	=>	10	12

Let us check with a program:

Program# 43

Addition of two matrices

```c
#include<stdio.h>

int main()
{
    int i, j;
    int row, col;
    int ar[10][10], br[10][10], cr[10][10];

    printf("How many rows ? ");
    scanf("%d", &row);

    printf("How many columns ? ");
    scanf("%d", &col);

    printf("Enter %d numbers for the first matrix now " , row*col);

    for(i = 0; i < row; i++)
        for(j = 0; j < col; j++)
            scanf("%d", &ar[i][j]);

    printf("Enter %d numbers for the second matrix now " , row*col);

    for(i = 0; i < row; i++)
        for(j = 0; j < col; j++)
            scanf("%d", &br[i][j]);

    for(i = 0; i < row; i++)
        for(j = 0; j < col; j++)
            cr[i][j] = ar[i][j] + br[i][j];

    printf("\nThe resultant matrix is \n");
```

```
for(i = 0; i < row; i++)
{
    for(j = 0; j < col ; j++)
        printf("%d\t", cr[i][j]);

    printf("\n");
}

return 0;
}
```

Run this program.

Multiplication of two matrices

Multiplication of matrices is only possible when the number of columns of the first matrix is equal to the number of rows of the second matrix. The multiplication can be done like this:

1	2		5	6		1x5+2x7	1x6+2x8		20	22
3	4	x	7	8	=	3x5+4x7	3x6+4x8	=>	43	50

If the first matrix is or order *m x n* and second matrix of order *n x p*, then the resultant matrix will be of order *m x p*.

Program# 44

Multiplication of two matrices

```c
#include<stdio.h>

int main()
{
    int i, j, k;
    int row1, col1, row2, col2;
    int ar[10][10], br[10][10], cr[10][10];

    printf("How many rows in first matrix ? ");
    scanf("%d", &row1);

    printf("How many columns in first matrix? ");
    scanf("%d", &col1);
```

```
    printf("The number of rows of second matrix is %d", col1);

    row2 = col1;

    printf("\nHow many columns in second matrix? ");
    scanf("%d", &col2);

    printf("Enter %d numbers for the first matrix now " , row1*col1);

    for(i = 0; i < row1; i++)
        for(j = 0; j < col1; j++)
            scanf("%d", &ar[i][j]);

    printf("Enter %d numbers for the second matrix now " , col1*col2);

    for(i = 0; i < row2; i++)
        for(j = 0; j < col2; j++)
            scanf("%d", &br[i][j]);

    /* multiply the matrices now */
    for(i = 0; i < row1; i++)
    {
        for( j = 0; j < col2; j++)
        {
            cr[i][j] = 0;
            for(k = 0; k <= col1 - 1; k++)
                cr[i][j] = cr[i][j] + ar[i][k] + br[k][j];
        }
    }

    printf("\nThe resultant matrix is \n");
    for(i = 0; i < row1; i++)
    {
        for(j = 0; j < col2; j++)
            printf("%d\t", cr[i][j]);

        printf("\n");
    }
    return 0;
}
```

Run this program.

Sum of diagonal of a matrix

We are now going to calculate the sum of numbers that lies on the two diagonals of the matrix. For example, if we have the matrix:

1	12	3
14	5	26
17	8	9

Then,   sum1 = 1 + 5 + 9 = 15

sum2 = 3 + 5 + 17 = 25

Program# 45

Sum of numbers on two diagonals

```c
#include<stdio.h>

int main()
{
    int i, j;
    int sum1 = 0, sum2 = 0;

    int row, col;

    int ar[10][10];

    printf("How many rows ? ");
    scanf("%d", &row);

    printf("How many columns ? ");
    scanf("%d", &col);

    printf("Enter %d numbers now\n", row * col);
    for(i = 0; i < row; i++)
        for(j = 0; j < col; j++)
            scanf("%d", &ar[i][j]);

    for(i = 0; i < row; i++)
    {
        for(j = 0; j < col; j++)
        {
            if(i == j)
                sum1 = sum1 + ar[i][j];
```

```c
            if(row - i - 1 == j)
                sum2 = sum2 + ar[i][j];
        }
    }

    printf("\nThe sum of numbers on first diagonal is %d", sum1);
    printf("\nThe sum of numbers on the second diagonal is %d", sum2);

    return 0;
}
```

Run this program.

SOLVED PROBLEMS

Q.1. What is index in an array?

Ans. Index is a number that identifies the position of an element in the array. The starting index in the array is always 0, the second element is at index 1, third is at index 2 and so on.

Q.2. Can an array have elements of different data types?

Ans. No, an array is a collection of similar type of elements.

Q.3. Can we initialize a 2D array without specifying its dimensions?

Ans. No, you must specify the second dimension.

```
/* Valid declaration*/
int arr[2][2] = {1, 2, 3 ,4 };
```

```
/* Valid declaration*/
int arr[][2] = {1, 2, 3 ,4 };
```

```
/* Invalid declaration - you must specify second dimension*/
int arr[][] = {1, 2, 3 ,4 }
```

```
/* Invalid because of the same reason mentioned above*/
int arr[2][] = {1, 2, 3 ,4 };
```

Q.4. Can we change the size of a 2D array at runtime?

Ans. If the array is declared statically, then we cannot change the size at runtime. But, if the array is declared dynamically using malloc, then we can change the size at runtime.

SOLVED PROGRAMS

Q.1. Write a program to check if a matrix is upper triangular matrix.

```
1    4    2
0    3    4
0    0    1
```

Logic: A square matrix is called an upper triangular matrix if all the entries below the main diagonal are 0.

```c
#include<stdio.h>
#include<stdlib.h>

int main()
{
    int i, j, n;
    int mat[10][10];

    printf("Enter number of rows/columns : ");
    scanf("%d", &n);

    if(n > 10)
    {
        printf("Maximum number of rows could be 10");
        exit(0);
    }

    printf("Enter %d numbers now\n", n*n);

    for(i = 0; i < n; i++)
    {
        for( j = 0; j < n; j++)
            scanf("%d", &mat[i][j]);
    }

    printf("The matrix is\n\n");
    for(i = 0; i < n; i++)
    {
        for(j = 0; j < n; j++)
```

```
            printf("%d\t", mat[i][j]);
                printf("\n");
    }

    for(i = 0; i < n; i++)
    {
        for(j = 0; j < n; j++)
        {
                if(i > j && mat[i][j] != 0)
                {
                        printf("Matrix is not upper triangular");
                        /* No need to go further, exit program */
                        exit(0);
                }
        }
    }

    printf("Matrix is upper triangular");

    return 0;
}
```

Run this program.

Q.2. Write a program to merge two arrays.

First array:	1 2 3 4 5
Second array:	6 7 8 9
Result:	1 2 3 4 5 6 7 8 9

Logic: Create a blank third array. First copy the elements of the first array in it and then append the elements of the second array.

```
#include<stdio.h>
#include<stdlib.h>

int main()
{
    int i, n1, n2;
    int ar[10], br[10], cr[20];
```

```c
printf("How many numbers to enter in first array : ");
scanf("%d", &n1);

if(n1 > 10)
{
    printf("Maximum number of elements can be 10");
    exit(0);
}

printf("Enter %d numbers now\n", n1);
for( i = 0; i < n1; i++)
    scanf("%d", &ar[i]);

printf("How many numbers to enter in second array : ");
scanf("%d", &n2);

if(n2 > 10)
{
    printf("Maximum number of elements can be 10");
    exit(0);
}

printf("Enter %d numbers now\n", n2);
for( i = 0; i < n2; i++)
    scanf("%d", &br[i]);

for(i = 0; i <= n1 + n2 - 1; i++)
{
    if(i < n1)
        cr[i] = ar[i];
    else
        cr[i] = br[i-n1];
}

printf("The resultant array is\n\n");
for(i = 0; i <= n1 + n2 - 1; i++)
    printf("%d\t", cr[i]);

return 0;
}
```

Run this program.

Q.3. Write a program to arrange negative numbers to one side and positive numbers to the other side of the array.

Input array: 4 -5 -9 34 12 -45

Result: -5 -9 -45 4 34 12

Logic: Initialize a positive number, find the first negative number and swap them.

```c
#include<stdio.h>
#include<stdlib.h>

int main()
{
    int i, j, n, temp, found;
    int ar[10];

    printf("How many numbers to enter in the array : ");
    scanf("%d", &n);

    if(n > 10)
    {
        printf("Maximum number of elements can be 10");
        exit(0);
    }

    printf("Enter %d numbers now\n", n);
    for(i = 0; i < n; i++)
        scanf("%d", &ar[i]);

    for(i = 0; i < n; i++)
    {
        /* positive found, now find first negative */
        if(ar[i] > 0)
        {
            found = 0;
            for(j = i + 1; j < n; j++)
            {
                if(ar[j] < 0)
                {
                    found = 1;
                    break;
                }
```

```c
        }
        if(found == 1)
        {
                temp = ar[i];
                ar[i] = ar[j];
                ar[j] = temp;
        }
    }
}

printf("The resultant array is\n\n");

for(i = 0; i < n; i++)
    printf("%d\t", ar[i]);

return 0;
}
```

Run this program.

Q.4. Program to fill a 2-D array in the following manner:

1	2	3	4
12	13	14	5
11	16	15	6
10	9	8	7

```c
#include<stdio.h>

int main()
{
   int i, j, k, n = 4, count = 0;
   int ar[4][4];

   /* initialize all numbers to 0 */
   for(i = 0; i < n; i++)
      for (j = 0; j < n; j++)
            ar[i][j] = 0;

   for(i = 0; i < n; i++)
```

```
{
    for(j = i; j < n - i; j++)
        ar[i][j] = ++count;

    for(j = i+1; j < n - i; j++)
        ar[j][n-i-1] = ++count;

    for(j = n-i-2; j >= i; j--)
        ar[n-i-1][j] = ++count;

    for(j = n-i-2; j > i; j--)
        ar[j][i] = ++count;
}
printf("The required array is\n");
for(i = 0; i < n; i++)
{
    for(j = 0; j < n; j++)
        printf("%d\t", ar[i][j]);

    printf("\n");
}

return 0;
}
```

Run this program.

UNSOLVED PROBLEMS

Q.1. What happens when the number of elements in the array exceeds the size of the array?

Q.2. How can you increase the size of an array at runtime?

Q.3. How do you copy an array to another array?

UNSOLVED PROGRAMS

Q.1. Calculate the sum of individual rows, columns and the two diagonals of a square matrix.

Q.2. Find all the prime numbers in an array.

Q.3. Copy an array to another array in reverse order.

Q.4. Input an array and rotate it the number of times specified by the user.

Q.5. Rotate a 2-D array by row and column.

Pointers are an extremely powerful programming tool. They can be used to dynamically allocate memory, which means we can write memory efficient programs.

Technically, a pointer represents the address (memory location) of a variable. We don't have to worry about the address value of a variable, pointer uses it internally.

A pointer can be declared like this:

```
int *p;
```

p is any name and *indicates pointer. At this moment, the pointer is of no use. To make this pointer point to a variable, we do:

```
int x;
p = &x;
```

The & operator indicates the address of the variable *x* here. The pointer *p* is ready to point to *x*. Now we can use the following statement to modify the value of *x* using pointer *p*:

```
*p = 10;                /*internally x = 10*/
```

Note

p represents address of the variable

*p represents the value of the variable.

Let us write a program that demonstrates the use of a pointer.

Program# 46

Demonstrate the user of pointer.

```c
#include<stdio.h>

int main()
{
    int a, b;
    int *p;

    printf("Enter number : ");
    scanf("%d", &a);

    p = &a;                 /* pointer points to variable a */

    printf("The square of %d is %d", a, *p * *p);

    printf("\nEnter another number : ");
    scanf("%d", &b);

    p = &b;                 /* now pointer points to variable b */

    printf("The square of %d is %d", *p, *p * *p);

    return 0;
}
```

Run this program.

Obviously the above program didn't show the actual use and strength of pointers. It simply demonstrates how we can use a pointer on different variables.

Fun with pointers

*p represents a pointer on some variable

```c
Ex. int x = 5;
    int *p = &x;        /* declare and initialize pointer */

    printf("Address of variable = %d", p);
    printf("\nValue of variable = %d", *p);
```

**p represents a pointer to a pointer, which in turn points to a variable

```
Ex.int x = 5;
   int *p = &x;
   int **t = &p;     /* t points to a pointer, for this, we used **   */

   printf("Value of original variable = %d", x);
   printf("\nValue of original variable using pointer = %d", *p);
   printf("\nValue of original variable through second pointer = %d", **t);
```

Note

We may be printing address of variable but actually, it is of no use to us at the moment.

Array & pointers

A pointer can be very useful with arrays. We can access an array using a pointer instead of an index. Also, pointer helps us to create dynamic memory for array (memory on demand) instead of static memory.

Addressing in array

An array is a collection of similar type of elements arranged in a linear way in memory. For example, an array of 5 integers can be represented like this:

ar[0]	ar[1]	ar[2]	ar[3]	ar[4]

Each memory block for the elements has 2 bytes of size. Hence, the size of array can be calculated as:

```
2 * sizeof(int) = 10 bytes
```

Here *sizeof()* is a built-in function that returns the size of data passed to it.

If we assume that the memory address of the first element is 1000, then we can find the memory address of other elements of array by adding 2 bytes. Thus, the array elements will have following memory locations:

```
   ar[0]       ->     1000
   ar[1]       ->     1002
   ar[2]       ->     1004
   ar[3]       ->     1006
   ar[4]       ->     1008
```

Accessing array elements through pointer

A pointer can be used to point to array. We can use a pointer to read array elements by shifting pointer by 2 bytes. For example:

```
int *p;
p = &ar[0];          /* pointer points to the first element of array */
                     /* we can also use p = ar */
```

At the moment, *p gives the value of ar[0]
If we add 2 bytes to pointer, we will get a second element:

```
p = p + 1;           /* pointer is shifted by 1*2 bytes because of int data type */
```

Hence, *p will give value of *ar[1]* this time.

Let us write a program to demonstrate how we can use a pointer to read array elements.

Program# 47

Using pointer to read array elements

```
#include<stdio.h>
#include<stdlib.h>

int main()
{
    int ar[10];
    int *p;
    int i, size;

    printf("How many numbers to enter in the array : ");
    scanf("%d", &size);

    if(size > 10)
    {
        printf("Maximum number of elements can be 10");
        exit(0);
    }

    printf("Enter %d numbers now\n", size);
    for(i = 0; i < size; i++)
    scanf("%d", &ar[i]);
```

```
    p = &ar[0];

    for(i = 0; i < size; i++)
    {
        printf("%d\t", *p);
        p = p + 1;                    /* or p++ */
    }

    return 0;
}
```

Run this program.

Dynamic memory allocation for array

We use to declare like this:

```
int ar[30];
```

The above statement declares an array of 30 elements. But what if we want to work with 5 elements only? The space of 25 elements goes waste. To avoid this wastage of memory, we have to create dynamic memory for array, i.e. memory on demand.

We can use a pointer to create dynamic memory for array with the help of built-in function *malloc()*.

An array of n elements can be created dynamically with the statements:

```
int *ar;

ar = (int*) malloc(n * sizeof(int));
```

    or

```
ar = (int*) malloc(n * 2);
```

So, before working on array, we can ask the user to enter the number of elements required in array and then we can create memory for those elements only.

Let us write a program to demonstrate the above discussion.

Program# 48

Create dynamic memory for array

```c
#include<stdio.h>
#include<stdlib.h>          /* for malloc function */

int main()
{
    int i, size;
    int *ar;

    printf("How many numbers to enter in the array : ");
    scanf("%d", &size);

    ar = (int*) malloc(size * sizeof(int));

    printf("Enter %d numbers now\n", size);
    for(i = 0; i < size; i++)
        scanf("%d", &ar[i]);

    printf("\nThe array is\n");

    for(i = 0; i < size; i++)
        printf("%d\t", ar[i]);

    return 0;
}
```

Run this program.

Array pointing to itself

If we remove the brackets of array, the array name becomes the pointer to the first element of the array. Hence, *ar* is same as *&ar[0]*.

So, if we have an array *ar*:

```c
int ar[5] = {1,2,3,4,5};
    int i, size = 5;
```

We may write a for loop to read values of the array like this:

```c
    for(i = 0; i < size; i++)
        printf("%d\t", ar[i]);
```

as well as:

```
for(i = 0; i < size; i++)
    printf("%d\t", *(ar + i));
```

To read values in array, we can write *scanf()* like this:

```
for(i = 0; i < size; i++)
    scanf("%d\t", ar + i);
```

Dynamic memory for 2-D arrays

In case of 2-D arrays, we have to specify the number of rows first and then dynamic memory for each row is created. Here is an example:

```
int *ar[10];   /* a 2-D array of 10 rows */

printf("How many columns in array ? ");
scanf("%d", &col);

for(i = 0; i < 10; i++)
ar[i] = (int*) malloc(col * sizeof(int));
```

UNSOLVED PROBLEMS

Q.1. What happens when the number of elements in array exceeds the size of the array?

Q.2. How can you increase the size of an array at runtime?

Q.3. How do you copy an array to another array?

Q.4. How can you access 2D array elements by using a pointer?

UNSOLVED PROGRAMS

Q.1. Calculate the sum of individual rows, columns and the two diagonals of a square matrix.

Q.2. Find all the prime numbers in an array.

Q.3. Copy an array to another array in reverse order.

Q.4. Input an array and rotate it the number of times specified by the user.

Q.5. Rotate a 2-D array by row and column.

Functions are one of the most important parts of any programming language. They allow us to re-use our code. With the help of functions, we can write clean and logical code and we can divide our program into smaller components which are easy to manage.

Writing big and complex programs without using functions is a very difficult task.

We have already used many functions previously like printf, scanf, etc.

A function can be declared with the following syntax:

```
return_type function_name(argument 1, argument 2 …)
{

}
```

Few points:-

- Function definition contains the body of function in which we write code.
- A function has a prototype (signature) that needs to be declared before we use them.
- A function call is a statement where we use the function in our code.
- We can send values to functions while calling them. These values are called function arguments.
- A function can receive values that are passed to it in variables called function parameters.
- A function may or may not return a value (return type). If the function doesn't return a value, its return type is marked as **void** (means nothing) otherwise return type is the data type of the value returned.

A function should be declared before we use them otherwise the compiler will throw error complaining function not found. For this, we can declare the function prototype before *main()* like this:

```
return_type function_name(argument 1, argument 2 …);
```

Let us check some sample programs to demonstrate how we can use functions.

Program# 49

A function that does not receive or return a value

```c
#include<stdio.h>

/* declare function prototype */
void say_hello();

int main()
{
    /* call our function */
    say_hello();

    return 0;
}

/* function definition */
void say_hello()
{
    printf("Hello from function");
}
```

Note

You can use any valid naming style for your functions. Some prefer to use underscore while others prefer camel case to name their functions. Hence, both naming styles are fine: say_hello() or sayHello()

How above program is executed:-

C executes our program from top to bottom.

When it finds that we are calling a function, it stops current function execution and jumps on to execute the called function.

Then it returns back to previous function and start executing the next line.

Here are the steps in which the above program is executed:

- Program execution starts with *main()*
- It finds function *clrscr()*
- It finds that clrscr() is defined in conio.h

- It executes the function, clears the screen and returns back to *main()*
- It then reads the next function *say_hello()*
- It finds the prototype of the function before main and jumps to the body of *say_hello()*
- It then finds the function *printf()*
- It finds the definition of this function in *stdio.h*, executes it, finds the end of *say_hello()* and returns to *main()*
- It finds the function *getch()*
- It finds the definition of getch() in *conio.h*, executes it and returns to main()
- It finally reaches the end and program stops

> **Note**
>
> If we write the function definition before main(), then we don't have to declare its prototype.

Passing values to functions

We can pass any type of values to functions. This allows us to change the calculation within the function based on the passed values.

Values can be passed to functions in two ways:

1. **Pass by value:**

In this method, a copy of the variable is passed to the called function. Changes made to the copy will not affect the original value of the variable.

2. **Pass by reference:**

In this method, we pass the location of variable instead of the value of variable. This allows us to work directly on the variable instead of its copy.

Pass by value examples

In the next example, we will see the behavior of pass by value.

Program# 50

A function that receives a single argument by value and returns nothing

```c
#include<stdio.h>

/* declare function prototype with parameter of type int */
void func(int);

int main()
```

```c
{
    int number = 5;

    printf("\nInitial value = %d", number);

    /* call our function and pass value of variable number */
    func(number);

    printf("\nValue now = %d", number);

    return 0;
}

/* number is the parameter which will receive copy of value of variable from main */
void func(int number)
{
    number = 10;
    printf("\nValue in function = %d", number);
}
```

After running the program, you will see the following output:

```
Initial value = 5
Value in function = 10
Value now = 5
```

Hence, passing the variable by value will not change the original value of variable *number* in *main()*.

Program# 51

A function that receives a single argument and returns nothing

```c
#include<stdio.h>

/* declare function prototype with parameter of type int */
void square(int);

int main()
{
    int number = 5;

    /* call our function and pass value of variable number */
    square(number);
```

```
    return 0;
}

/* function body, number is parameter which will receive the value 5 */
void square(int number)
{
    printf("Square of %d is %d", number, number * number);
}
```

Run this program.

Program# 52

A function that receives two arguments and returns nothing

```
#include<stdio.h>

/* declare function prototype that receives two integer values */
void add(int, int);

int main()
{
    /* call the function */
    add(5, 6);

    return 0;
}
/* create function body */
void add(int number1, int number2)
{
    printf("Sum of %d and %d is %d", number1, number2, number1 + number2);
}
```

Run this program.

Program# 53

A function that receives two arguments and returns an integer

```c
#include<stdio.h>

/* declare function prototype that receives two integer values and returns integer */

int sum(int, int);
int main()
{
    /* call our function, get the returned value in variable result */
    int result = sum(5, 6);

    printf("Sum of numbers = %d", result);

    return 0;
}

/* function body with two parameters */
int sum(int number1, int number2)
{
    return number1 + number2;
}
```

Run this program.

Pass by reference examples

When we pass a variable by reference, we are actually passing its location (or address) instead of value. To read the location, we need a pointer with the help of which we can extract the value of that location.

Since we can access the memory location of the variable, hence, we can change the value of the original variable as well.

To pass a variable by reference, we use & sign telling that we want to pass location instead of value.

Here is a program that demonstrates the use of pass by reference.

Program# 54

A function that receives a single argument by value and returns nothing

```c
#include<stdio.h>

/* function prototype with parameter of type int pointer */
void func(int*);

int main()
{
    int number = 5;

    printf("\nInitial value = %d", number);

    /* call our function and pass value of variable number */
    func(&number);

    printf("\nValue now = %d", number);

    return 0;
}

/* number is the pointer parameter which receives location of variable from main */
void func(int* number)
{
    /* Change value of variable using pointer */
    *number = 10;

    printf("\nValue in function = %d", *number);
}
```

After running the program, you will see the following output:

```
Initial value = 5
Value in function = 10
Value now = 10
```

Hence, passing the variable by reference will allow the function to change the value of the original variable.

Program# 55

Calculate square and cube of a number without returning anything from function

```c
#include<stdio.h>

/* function prototype that receives one integer value and two memory locations */
void calculate(int, int*, int*);

int main()
{
    int number = 5;
    int square, cube;

    /* call our function, pass number by value, square & cube by reference */
    calculate(number, &square, &cube);

    printf("Square of %d is %d", number, square);
    printf("\nCube of %d is %d", number, cube);

    return 0;

}

/* Receive one integer value and two references */
void calculate(int number, int* square, int* cube)
{
    /* Change values of variables declared in main() */
    *square = number * number;
    *cube = number * number * number;
}
```

Run this program.

Note

It is not necessary to give the same names to parameters and arguments, but, it is always a good practice to use similar names so that we don't have to remember a lot of names.

Passing array to function

Actually we cannot pass an array to a function. Wait what?

Yes, array is a sequence of memory and passing array means passing all the memory to the function.

Instead, we pass only the location of the first element in the array. Then we can read the full array by reading consecutive memories.

Here is an example that shows how to pass the array location to function.

Program# 56

A function that receives an array and prints it

```c
#include<stdio.h>

/* function prototype that receives location and size of array */
void print_array(int[], int);

int main()
{
    int ar[] = {7, 4, 8, 3, 5};

    /* pass location of first array element and size of array */
    /* ar[0] is the first array element, &ar[0] is its location in memory */
    print_array (&ar[0], 5);

    return 0;
}
void print_array(int ar[], int size)
{
    int i;

    for(i = 0; i < size; i++)
    {
        printf("%d ", ar[i]);
    }
}
```

> **Note**
>
> Array name itself is the location of the first element in the array, hence:
>
> *ar* and & *ar[0]* are both the same.
>
> Similarly:
>
> *ar+1* and & *ar[1]* are the same
>
> *ar+2* and & *ar[2]* are the same etc.
>
> In the previous program, we may also call *print_array* function like this:
>
> ```
> print_array(ar, 5);
> ```

> **Note**
>
> Since we are passing memory location of first element of the array, we can also use pointer as a parameter like this:
>
> ```
> void print_array(int* ar, int size)
> ```
>
> Rest of the program remains the same

Returning arrays from function

Again, we return the location of the first array element from the function instead of returning the whole memory.

Here is an example that generates an array with random numbers.

Program# 57

Generate an array with random numbers

```
/***********************************************
Steps we need to do for this program
1. Ask user how many numbers to generate
2. Generate array with random numbers of given size
3. Print the array

***********************************************/

#include<stdio.h>
#include<stdlib.h>      /* for random function */
```

```c
/* function prototype that receives size of array and returns array */
int* get_random_array(int);

/* function prototype that returns an integer */
int get_array_size();

/* function prototype that prints the array with random numbers */
void print_array(int*, int);

int main()
{
    int* ar;
    int size;

    /* Ask for array size */
    size = get_array_size();

    if(size < 1)
    {
        printf("Invalid size");
        exit(0);    /* terminate program */
    }

    /* generate random numbers */
    ar = get_random_array(size);

    /* print generated array */
    print_array(ar, size);

    return 0;
}

/* get size of array from user */
int get_array_size()
{
    int size;

    printf("How many numbers you want to generate? ");
    scanf("%d", &size);

    return size;
}
```

```
/* generate random numbers in array and return */
int* get_random_array(int size)
{
    /* We will generate random numbers between 1-100 */
    int i;
    int* ar = (int*) malloc(size * sizeof(int));

    for(i = 0; i < size; i++)
        ar[i] = random() % 100 + 1;

    return ar;
}

void print_array(int* ar, int size)
{
    int i;

    for(i = 0; i < size; i++)
        printf("%d ", ar[i]);
}
```

Recursion

Recursion is a process in which a function calls itself. This is done to repeat execution of function until a condition is met.

Recursive functions are very useful in solving various repetitive problems.

Here is an example of a function calling itself to calculate the factorial of a number.

Program# 58

Calculate the factorial of a function using recursion

```
#include<stdio.h>

int factorial(int);
int get_number();

int main()
{
    int number, result;
```

```
    number = get_number();

    result = factorial (number);

    printf("Factorial of %d is %d", number, result);

    return 0;
}
int get_number()
{
    int number;

    printf("Enter number for factorial: ");
    scanf("%d", &number);

    return number;
}
int factorial (int number)
{
    if(number > 0)
        return number * factorial (number - 1);
    else
        return 1;
}
```

If the input number is 5, the program execution will work like this:

```
5 * factorial(4)
5 * 4 * factorial(3)
...
5* 4 * 3 * 2 * 1
```

How Recursion Works?

Recursion works on a recursive stack. So, whenever a function is called recursively, all the statements within the function are put on the stack and then popped one by one.

Here is an example:

```
void func_recursive(int n)
{
    if(n == 0)
    return; /* Skip next lines, finishes the function execution */

    func_recursive(n-1);
    printf("%d\n", n);
}
```

Now call this function like this:

```
func_recursive(3);
```

What will be the output from the above function?

Value is never printed? Wrong!

Here is what will happen in each run:

Step 1:

```
    func_recursive(3);
```

Result on stack:

```
    if(3 == 0) ..

    func_recursive(2);

    printf(3)
```

On execution, the first statement popped will be *if(..)* which returns false

The second line *func_recursive(2)* is again a recursive call, hence it will generate new values on stack.

Step 2:

```
    func_recursive(2)
```

Result on stack:

```
    if(2 == 0) ..
    func_recursive(1)
    printf(2)
    printf(3)   <= this statement already exist on stack waiting to be executed
```

Step 3:

```
func_recursive(1)
```

Result on stack:

```
if(1 == 0)..
func_recursive(0)
printf(1)
printf(2)
printf(3)
```

Step 4:

```
if(0 == 0) ..
printf(1)
printf(2)
printf(3)
```

No func_recursive(-1) will be called as the condition if(0 == 0) will terminate the function call. Now, popping statements one by one, the final result will be:

```
1
2
3
```

What will happen if the function is like this?

```
void func_recursive(int n)
{
   if(n == 0)
      return;     /* Skip next lines, finishes the function execution */

   printf("%d\n", n);
   func_recursive(n-1);
}
```

The stack will be like this:

```
if(3 == 0) ..
printf(3)
func_recursive(2)
```

The final result will be:

```
3
2
1
```

Let us see one more interesting example:-

Program# 59

A more interesting recursion demo

```c
#include<stdio.h>

void func_recursive(int);

int main()
{
   func_recursive(3);
   return 0;
}

void func_recursive(int n)
{
   if(n == 0)
      return;

   func_recursive(n-1);
   printf("\n%d", n);
   func_recursive(n-1);
}
```

Macros

Macros are identifiers that can have expressions or group of statements. A macro can be declared using the #define statement.

Examples of macros are:

```c
#define PI 3.142
#define square(n) ( n* n)
#define MIN(a, b) ( a < b ? a : b)
```

Program# 60

A program showing how to use macro

```c
#include<stdio.h>

#define PI 3.142

#define MIN(a, b) (a < b ? a : b)
#define circle_area(radius) (PI * radius * radius)

int main()
{
    double area, radius = 7;

    area = circle_area(radius);

    printf("Area of square with radius %.2lf is %.2lf", radius, area);

    printf("\nMinimum of %d and %d is %d", 4,7, MIN(4, 7));

    printf("\nMinimum of %f and %f is %f", 5.6,7.2, MIN(5.6, 7.2));

    return 0;
}
```

Run this program.

How macros are different from functions?

Macros are **pre-processed** which means that all the macros would be processed before your program compiles. However, functions are not preprocessed but compiled.

Whenever a function is called, the call is transferred to the body of the function and after executing the body, returns back.

Whenever a macro is called, the code of macro is replaced at the place of call instead of transferring the call.

Macros make the program more readable and efficient but make sure your macros are small.

Predefined Macros

C language provides predefined macros to use. Following are few commonly used macros:

__DATE__   Represents current date in MMM DD YYYY format

__TIME__   Represents current time in HH:MM:SS format

__FILE__   Represents current file name

Program# 61

A program to show use of predefined macros

```c
#include<stdio.h>

int main()
{

    printf("%s", __DATE__);
    printf("\n%s", __TIME__);
    printf("\n%s", __FILE__);

    return 0;
}
```

String basics

A string is a collection or array of characters. Examples of string are:

```
"Ruchira", "Sanjay", "12ab", "abc@def", etc.
```

A string is always terminated by a special character \0. While reading a string character by character, we can always check this character for end. We need to use %s to input or output strings as a whole, we don't have to manage them character by character.

A string looks like this:

```
name = "Ayushman";

name[0] = 'A'
name[1] = 'y'
name[2] = 'u'
name[3] = 's'
name[4] = 'h'
name[5] = 'm'
name[6] = 'a'
name[7] = 'n'
name[8] = '\0'
```

Declaring a string

A string can be declared in following ways:

```
char name[50];
```

Initialize a string

A string can be initialized in following ways:

```
char name[50] = "This is a string";
```

        or

```
char name[] = "This is a string";        /* no need to specify size */
```

or

```
char *name = "This is a string";
```

Here is a program that demonstrates the use of strings:

Program# 62

A program showing how to use strings

```
#include<stdio.h>
#include<string.h>

int main()
{
    char name[50];
    char str1[] = "This is a string";        /* no need to specify size */
    char *str2 = "This is a string";

    printf("Enter your name : ");
    scanf("%s", name);

    printf("\nHello %s", name);
    printf("\nFirst initialized string = %s", str1);
    printf("\nSecond initialized string = %s", str2);

    return 0;
}
```

Run this program.

Print a string character by character

To print a string character by character, we can use a loop like this:

```
i = 0;
while(name[i] != '\0')
{
    printf("%c", name[i]);
    i++;
}
```

Input multiple words in a string

When we use *scanf()* with *%s* to read a string, it reads until it encounters a space. Give it a try and enter *India is big*:

```
char str[50];
printf("Enter a string with spaces: ");
scanf("%s", str);
printf("%s", str);
```

The output will be *India*

Now change *scanf()* to the following statement:

```
scanf("%[^\n]", str);
```

This tells **C** to read input until *\n* (enter key) character is encountered. Similarly, we can tell **C** to read until a $ character is encountered with the following statement:

```
scanf("%[^$]", str);
```

Passing string to function

A string can be passed to a function in the same way we pass an array to function. Here is a program to show how we can pass a string to function:

Program# 63

A program showing how to use strings

```
#include<stdio.h>

/* function prototype that accepts a string */
void say_hello(char*);

int main()
{
  char name[50];

  printf("Enter your name : ");
  scanf("%s", name);

  say_hello(name);

  return 0;
}
```

```
void say_hello(char *name)
{
    printf("Hello %s", name);
}
```

Run this program.

In-built string functions

There are various string functions provided by **C** that we can use in our programs. To use string functions, we have to include the header file *string.h*.

Here are some common string functions that we can use in our programs:

1. **strlen(char *str)**

   Returns length of the passed string (excluding \0 character)

   Example:

   ```
   length = strlen("India is big");
   ```

2. **strcat(char *string1, char *string2)**

   Combines string1 and string2 into string1

   Example:

   ```
   char str1[] = "Hello";
   char str2[] = "World";
   strcat(str1, str2);
   ```

3. **strncat(char *destination, char *source, int length)**

   Combines specified number of characters of string1 and string2 into string1

   Example:

   ```
   char str1[] = "Hello world";
   char str2[] = "This is great";
   strcat(str1, str2, 5);
   ```

4. **strcmp(char *string1, char *string2)**

   Compares two strings with following return conditions:

   - Returns 0 if the strings are equal
   - Returns the difference of the ASCII values of the characters that do not much

Example:

```
char str1[] = "joy";
char str2[] = "boy";
result = strcmp(str1, str2);
```

5. **strncmp(char *string1, char *string2, int length)**

   Compares specified number of characters of two strings with following return conditions:

   - Used to compare specified number of characters
   - Returns 0 if strings are equal
   - Returns the difference of the ASCII values of the characters that do not much

   Example:

   ```
   char str1[] = "joy";
   char str2[] = "boy";
   result = strncmp(str1, str2);
   ```

6. **strrev(char *str)**

   Reverses the passed string

   Example:

   ```
   char str[] = "joy";
   strrev(str);
   ```

7. **strcpy(char *destination, char *source)**

   Copies one string to another

   Example:

   ```
   strcpy("Reena", str);
   ```

8. **strncpy(char *destination, char *source, int length)**

   Copies defined number of characters of one string to another string

   Example:

   ```
   char str_source[] = "How are you?";
   char str_dest[50];
   strncpy(str_dest, str_source, 5);
   ```

9. **strupr(char *str)**

   Converts characters in string to uppercase

Example:

```
char str[] = "hello world";
strupr(str);
```

10. strlwr(char *str)

Converts characters in string to lowercase

Example:

```
char str[] = "HELLO WORLD";
strupr(str);
```

11. gets(str)

Inputs a string from the keyboard until the enter key is pressed.

Example:

```
char str[50];
printf("Enter a string: ");
gets(str);
```

12. puts(str)

Prints a string to the output screen and moves cursor to the next line.

Example:

```
char name[] = "This is a test string";
puts(name);
```

Array of strings

To manage multiple strings, we can use an array of strings. The array is a 2-dimensional array of characters where each row represents a single string.

Array of strings can be declared like this:

```
char names[5][40];
```

Here first dimension [5] represents the number of strings whereas the second dimension [40] represents maximum length of each string.

To initialize an array of strings, we can write:

```
char names[3][20] = {"Shaurya", "Prisha", "Urvashi"};
```

or

```
/* no need to specify number of strings */
char *names[20] = {"Shaurya", "Prisha", "Urvashi"};
```

This will result in:

```
names[0] = "Shaurya"
names[1] = "Prisha"
names[2] = "Urvashi"
```

Program# 64

Program to work with array of strings

```c
#include<stdio.h>

int main()
{
    int count, i;
    char names[10][50];

    printf("How many names you want to enter ?  ");
    scanf("%d", &count);

    printf("\nEnter %d names now\n", count);
    for(i=0; i<count; i++)
    {
        /* space before % to ignore enter key from buffer */
        scanf(" %[^\n]", names[i]);
    }

    printf("Now printing the strings you entered\n");
    for(i=0; i<count; i++)
    {
        printf("%s\n", names[i]);
    }

    return 0;
}
```

Run this program.

Passing array of strings to function

To pass an array of string to a function, pass the location of the first string in the array, which is the name of the array itself. Here is the above program using function:

Program# 65

Program to pass an array of strings to function

```c
#include<stdio.h>

void fun_str(char names[][50], int count);

int main()
{
    int count, i;
    char names[10][50];

    printf("How many names you want to enter ?  ");
    scanf("%d", &count);

    printf("\nEnter %d names now\n", count);
    for(i=0; i<count; i++)
    {
        /* space before % to ignore enter key from buffer */
        scanf(" %[^\n]", names[i]);
    }

    fun_str(names, count);

    return 0;
}

void fun_str(char names[][50], int count)
{
    int i;

    printf("Now printing the strings you entered\n");
    for(i=0; i<count; i++)
    {
        printf("%s\n", names[i]);
    }
}
```

Run this program.

CHAPTER 10

STRUCTURES & UNIONS

Introduction to structures

In the real world, data is not defined as int, float, char type of variables. Instead, we use them as employee, car, student, etc. To implement such functionality in programming, we need to group our data types.

Structures are used to group simple data types to create meaningful and complex types. The syntax of a structure is:

```
struct name_of_structure
{
    ----------------------;
    variable declarations;
    ----------------------;
};
```

Here is an example of a structure:

```
struct employee
{
    int id;
    float salary;
    char name[50];
};
```

A structure is only a definition and has no memory. The memory is created for structure type variables like this:

```
struct employee e1, e2;
```

Here we have created two employee type variables. Both *e1* and *e2* will have their separate memory space, which is the total of memory of its variables.

```
memory of e1 = sizeof(id) + sizeof(salary) + sizeof(name)
memory of e2 = sizeof(id) + sizeof(salary) + sizeof(name)
```

Now we can set values for the structure type variables like this:

```
e1.id = 1;
strcpy(e1.name, "Archana");
e1.salary = 40000;

e2.id = 2;
strcpy(e2.name, "Javed");
e2.salary = 30000;
```

Let us check an example to see how structure works.

Program# 66

To demonstrate the working of structures

```c
#include<stdio.h>

struct employee
{
    int id;
    float salary;
    char name[50];
};

int main()
{
    struct employee emp;

    printf("Enter id : ");
    scanf("%d", &emp.id);

    printf("Enter name : ");
    getchar();            /* Remove \n character left in input buffer */
    scanf("%s", &emp.name);

    printf("Enter salary : ");
    scanf("%f", &emp.salary);
```

```
printf("\nHere is the data you entered\n");
printf("\nId = %d", emp.id);
printf("\nName = %s", emp.name);
printf("\nSalary = %f", emp.salary);

return 0;
}
```

Run this program.

Initializing structure variables

A structure variable can be declared like this:

```
struct employee emp = { 1, "Sumit", 20000 };
```

This will set the following variables of *emp*:

```
emp.id = 1
emp.name = "Sumit"
emp.salary = 20000
```

> **Note**
>
> The values to be initialized must be placed in the same order as order of variables defined in the structure.

Array of structures

To create multiple structure type variables, we can declare an array of structure variables. This can be done in the same way as we have used normal arrays.

Let us check an example to see how we can use an array of structure variables:

Program# 67

Working with an array of structures

```c
#include<stdio.h>
struct employee
{
  int id;
  float salary;
  char name[50];
};

int main()
{
  int i, count;
  struct employee employees[50];

  printf("How many employees you want to enter? ");
  scanf("%d", &count);

  for(i = 0; i < count; i++)
  {
    printf("\nRecord# %d", i+1);
    printf("\nEnter id : ");
    scanf("%d", &employees[i].id);

    printf("Enter name : ");
    getchar();        /* Remove \n character left in input buffer */
    scanf("%s", & employees[i].name);

    printf("Enter salary : ");
    scanf("%f", & employees[i].salary);
  }
  printf("\nHere is the data you entered\n");
  for(i = 0; i < count; i++)
  {
    printf("\nRecord# %d", i+1);
    printf("\nId = %d", employees[i].id);
    printf("\nName = %s", employees[i].name);
```

```
        printf("\nSalary = %0.2f", employees[i].salary);
        printf("\n--------------------");
    }
    return 0;
}
```

Run this program.

Dynamic memory for array of structures

We have a bad programming statement in the previous program:

```
struct employee employees[50];
```

This statement creates 50 structure type variables without asking how many we want. For example, if we want to create only 2 variables, then memory of 48 structure variables goes waste.

We will make the following changes to the previous program to make sure we create only that much memory that we require.

Now, declare array of structures like this:

```
struct employee *employees;
```

Create memory for structure array like this:

```
employees = (struct employee*) malloc(sizeof(struct employee));
```

Here is the updated program:

Program# 68

Creating dynamic memory for an array of structures

```
#include<stdio.h>
#include<stdlib.h>

struct employee
{
    int id;
    float salary;
    char name[50];
};
```

```c
int main()
{
    int i, count;
    struct employee *employees;

    printf("How many employees you want to enter? ");
    scanf("%d", &count);

    employees = (struct employee*) malloc(sizeof(struct employee));

    for(i = 0; i < count; i++)
    {
        printf("\nRecord# %d", i+1);
        printf("\nEnter id : ");
        scanf("%d", &employees[i].id);

        printf("Enter name : ");
        /* Remove \n character left in input buffer */
        getchar();
        scanf("%s", & employees[i].name);

        printf("Enter salary : ");
        scanf("%f", & employees[i].salary);
    }

    printf("\nHere is the data you entered\n");

    for(i = 0; i < count; i++)
    {
        printf("\nRecord# %d", i+1);
        printf("\nId = %d", employees[i].id);
        printf("\nName = %s", employees[i].name);
        printf("\nSalary = %0.2f", employees[i].salary);
        printf("\n-------------------");
    }

    return 0;
}
```

Run this program.

Passing structures to functions

Structures can be passed to functions just like normal variables: *pass by value* or *pass by reference*. We have already learned the difference between pass by value and pass by reference.

The following two programs will demonstrate the two methods of passing structures to functions:

Program# 69

Pass structure to function by value

```c
#include<stdio.h>
#include<string.h>

struct employee
{
    int id;
    float salary;
    char name[50];
};

/* declare the function prototype */
void show_info(struct employee);

int main()
{
    struct employee emp;

    printf("Enter id : ");
    scanf("%d", &emp.id);

    printf("Enter name : ");
    getchar();                 /* Remove \n character left in input buffer */
    scanf("%s", &emp.name);

    printf("Enter salary : ");
    scanf("%f", &emp.salary);

    show_info(emp);

    printf("\n\nInformation from main\n");
    printf("\nId = %d", emp.id);
    printf("\nName = %s", emp.name);
```

```c
    printf("\nSalary = %0.2f", emp.salary);

    return 0;
}

void show_info(struct employee emp)
{
    printf("\nInformation from function\n");
    printf("\nId = %d", emp.id);
    printf("\nName = %s", emp.name);
    printf("\nSalary = %0.2f", emp.salary);

    /* try to change value of emp */
    emp.id = 100;
    strcpy(emp.name, "Someone");
    emp.salary = 0;
}
```

Run this program.

Program# 70

Pass structure to function by reference

```c
#include<stdio.h>
#include<string.h>

struct employee
{
    int id;
    float salary;
    char name[50];
};

/* declare the function prototype */
void show_info(struct employee*);

int main()
{
    struct employee emp;

    printf("Enter id : ");
    scanf("%d", &emp.id);
```

```c
    printf("Enter name : ");
    getchar();                      /* Remove \n character left in input buffer */
    scanf("%s", &emp.name);

    printf("Enter salary : ");
    scanf("%f", &emp.salary);

    show_info(&emp);

    printf("\n\nInformation from main\n");
    printf("\nId = %d", emp.id);
    printf("\nName = %s", emp.name);
    printf("\nSalary = %0.2f", emp.salary);

    return 0;
}

void show_info(struct employee *emp)
{
    printf("\nInformation from function\n");
    printf("\nId = %d", (*emp).id);
    printf("\nName = %s", (*emp).name);
    printf("\nSalary = %0.2f", (*emp).salary);

    /* try to change value of emp */
    (*emp).id = 100;
    strcpy((*emp).name, "Someone");
    (*emp).salary = 0;
}
```

Run this program.

> **Note**
>
> The statement:
>
> (*emp).id = 100;
>
> can also be written as:
>
> emp->id = 100;

The updated function looks like this:

```
void show_info(struct employee *emp)
{
    printf("\nInformation from function\n");
    printf("\nId = %d", emp->id);
    printf("\nName = %s", emp->name);
    printf("\nSalary = %0.2f", emp->salary);

    /* try to change value of emp */
    emp->id = 100;
    strcpy(emp->name, "Someone");
    emp->salary = 0;
}
```

Define our own data types

C provides keyword *typedef* to let us create our own data types. Actually, it allows us to give logical names to existing types. This makes the program more readable and logical.

For example, instead of:

```
int red, green, blue;
```

we can do:

```
typedef int color;          /* color will behave like int */
color red, green, blue;
```

Similarly, we can rename our structures to more logical names as well.

For example, instead of:

```
struct date
{
    int day, month, year;
};
```

we can write:

```
typedef struct
{
    int day, month, year;
}date;
```

Now we can create our structure variables like this:

```
date today;
```

instead of:

```
struct date today;
```

Union

A *union* is very similar to a structure with one major difference, memory management. The memory occupied by structure is the total of memories of all its members whereas the size of a union is the size of the variable with the biggest memory.

```
struct employee
{
    int id;
    float salary;
    char name[50];
};
```

Size of structure = sizeof(id) + sizeof(salary) + sizeof(name)

```
union employee
{
    int id;
    float salary;
    char name[50];
};
```

Size of union = sizeof(name)

When should I use a Union?

Use a union when you want to use one of its members at a time and memory conservation is a requirement.

Self-referential structures

A self-referential structure has a pointer member of its own type. Such type of structure is heavily used in data structures for creating linked lists, trees, etc.

Here is an example:

```
struct node
{
    int value;
    struct node *next;
};
```

We will see the use of such a structure in the chapter *Data Structures*.

Nested structures

We can declare one structure into another structure. This allows us to create more logical data types. Here is an example:

```
typedef struct
{
    int day, month, year;
}date;

typedef struct
{
    int id;
    float salary;
    char name[50];

    date date_of_birth;
}employee;
```

Let us check nested structures with a program:

Program# 71

To demonstrate the working of nested structures

```
#include<stdio.h>

typedef struct
{
    int day, month, year;

}date;

typedef struct
{
    int id;
```

```c
    float salary;
    char name[50];

    date date_of_birth;
}employee;

int main()
{
    employee emp;

    printf("Enter id : ");
    scanf("%d", &emp.id);

    printf("Enter name : ");
    getchar();              /* Remove \n character left in input buffer */
    scanf("%s", &emp.name);

    printf("Enter salary : ");
    scanf("%f", &emp.salary);

    printf("Enter date of birth:\n");
    printf("Day:\n");
    scanf("%d", &emp. date_of_birth.day);
    printf("Month:\n");
    scanf("%d", &emp.date_of_birth.month);
    printf("Year:\n");
    scanf("%d", &emp. date_of_birth.year);

    printf("\nHere is the data you entered\n");
    printf("\nId = %d", emp.id);
    printf("\nName = %s", emp.name);
    printf("\nSalary = %f", emp.salary);
    printf("\nDate of birth = %d/%d/%d",

    emp.date_of_birth.day, emp.date_of_birth.month, emp.date_of_birth.year);

    return 0;
}
```

Run this program.

If we need to initialize a nested structure, we can do it like this:

```c
employee emp = { 1, "Shubha", 50000, { 9, 8, 1995 } };
```

UNSOLVED PROBLEMS

Q.1. When do we need to declare one structure inside another structure?

Q.2. Is *struct* keyword compulsory to use?

UNSOLVED PROGRAMS

Q.1. Write a program to input marks of 5 subjects of 4 students. Find the students with the highest and lowest marks.

Q.2. Write a program to copy the contents of one structure to another using both pass by value and pass by reference methods.

Q.3. Write a program to enter employees in an array and sort them according to their date of birth.

Q.4. Write a program that will enter employees with following details:
id, name, post, salary
Now, ask user to enter post and print all employees matching the post.

Introduction to files

While writing programs, we may need to store program data permanently. To store data in files, C provides various functions that we can use in our programs.

Type of files

There are two types of files we can use in C:

1. Text Files

   In a text file, we write data in the form of characters. This type of file is used when we want to store text data to file.

2. Binary Files

   In a binary file, we write data in the form of bytes. This type of file is mostly used when we want to store integers, floats, structures, etc.

Text Files

Since a file represents memory on disk, we need a *FILE* type pointer to access it. To work with text files, we need to perform the following steps:

1. Declare FILE type pointer
   ```
   FILE *file;
   ```

2. Open the file for reading or writing
   ```
   file = fopen(filename, filemode)
   ```

3. Read or write data to file

4. Close the file
   ```
   fclose(file);
   ```

A file can be opened for reading, writing or appending.

Following are the modes in which we can open a file in text mode:

Mode	Description
r	Open text file for reading
w	Open text file for writing
a	Open text file for appending
r+	Open text file for reading and writing. Does not create a new file if the file does not exist. Does not delete the contents of existing files.
w+	Open text file for reading and writing. Creates a new file if the file does not exist. Deletes contents of existing file.
a+	Open text file for reading and writing. Creates a new file if the file does not exist. Writes at the end of existing file.

Functions to write data in files

Following are the functions we can use for reading or writing data to file:

1. fputc()

    This function is used to write single characters to the file. It returns the character written to the file or EOF in case of error.

2. putc()

    Similar to fputc() but can write to any output stream.

3. fputs()

    Similar to fputc() but can write to any output stream.

4. fprintf()

    Writes formatted data to file.

5. fwrite()

    Commonly used to write binary data to file.

Functions to read data from files

1. int fgetc()

    This function reads a single character from the file and moves to the next character.

2. getc()

    Similar to fgetc() but can read from any input stream.

3. gets()

> Reads specified number of characters from file to a character array. If this function encounters a newline character \n or the end of the file *EOF* while reading, it returns only the characters read up to that point, including the new line character.

4. fscanf()

> Reads formatted data from file.

5. fread()

> Commonly used to read binary data from file.

Program# 72

Read a text file character by character

```c
#include <stdio.h>
#include <stdlib.h>

int main()
{
    char ch;
    FILE *file;

    file = fopen("test.txt", "r");  /* open file for reading */

    if (file == NULL)
    {
        printf("Cannot open the file");
        exit(0);
    }

    printf("The contents of file are:\n");

    while((ch = fgetc(file)) != EOF)
            printf("%c", ch);

    fclose(file);

    printf("\nData reading complete");

    return 0;
}
```

Run this program.

> **Note**
>
> Make sure you have the file *test.txt* in the directory from where your C program is running or give some other path like this: *c:\\files\\test.txt*

Program# 73

Write characters in a text file

```c
#include <stdio.h>
#include <stdlib.h>

int main()
{
    int i;
    FILE *file;
    char string[] = "This is some text to write in file";

    file = fopen("data.txt", "w");         /* open file for writing*/

    if (file == NULL)
    {
        printf("Cannot open the file");
        exit(0);
    }

    for(i = 0; string[i]!='\0'; i++)
        fputc(string[i], file);

    fclose(file);

    printf("\nData writing complete");

    return 0;
}
```

Run this program.

Program# 74

Read a file line by line

```c
#include <stdio.h>
#include <stdlib.h>

int main()
{
    FILE *file;
    char string[256];

    file = fopen("test.txt", "r");        /* open file for reading */

    if (file == NULL)
    {
        printf("Cannot open the file");
        exit(0);
    }

    printf("The contents of file are:\n");

    while(fgets(string, sizeof(string), file))
        printf("%s\n", string);

    fclose(file);

    printf("\nData reading complete");

    return 0;
}
```

Run this program.

Program# 75

Write string to a file

```c
#include <stdio.h>
#include <stdlib.h>

int main()
{
   int i;
   FILE *file;
   char string[256] = "This is a line\nThis is another line";

   file = fopen("data.txt", "w");  /* open file for writing*/

   if (file == NULL)
   {
      printf("Cannot open the file");
      exit(0);
   }

   fputs(string, file);

   fclose(file);

   printf("\nData writing complete");

   return 0;
}
```

Run this program.

Program# 76

Write formatted data to file

```c
#include <stdio.h>
#include <stdlib.h>

int main()
{
   int age;
   FILE *file;
```

```c
    char name[50], gender[10];

    file = fopen("test.txt", "w");  /* open file for writing */

    if (file == NULL)
    {
        printf("Cannot open the file");
        exit(0);
    }

    printf("Enter your name: ");
    scanf("%[^\n]", name);           /* Read until the enter key is found */

    printf("Enter your age :");
    scanf("%d", &age);

    /* clear enter key */
    getchar();

    printf("Enter your gender (male/female/other) :");
    scanf("%s", gender);

    printf("\nNow writing data to file\n");

    /* Write to file separating each variable by a tab */
    fprintf(file, "%s\t%d\t%s", name, age, gender);

    fclose(file);

    printf("\nData writing complete");

    return 0;
}
```

Run this program.

Now we will read text file created by above program.

Program# 77

Read formatted data from file

```c
#include <stdio.h>
#include <stdlib.h>

int main()
{
    int age;
    FILE *file;
    char name[50], gender[10];

    file = fopen("test.txt", "r");  /* open file for reading */

    if (file == NULL)
    {
        printf("Cannot open the file");
        exit(0);
    }

    printf("Now reading data from file\n");

    /* Read until tab character is encountered */
    fscanf(file, "%[^\t] %d %s", name, &age, gender);

    printf("\nName: %s", name);
    printf("\nAge: %d", age);
    printf("\nGender: %s", gender);

    fclose(file);

    printf("\nData reading complete");

    return 0;
}
```

Run this program.

Binary Files

Binary files manipulate data in the form of bytes instead of characters. Writing binary data give us more control in managing data in files. For example:

If we write 12345 as text, it will take 5 bytes (characters have size of 1 byte)

If we write 12345 as binary data (int), it will take 2 bytes in memory

Following are the modes in which we can open a file in binary mode:

Mode	Description
rb	Open file for reading
wb	Open file for writing
ab	Open file for appending
rb+	Open file for reading and writing. Does not create a new file if the file does not exist. Does not delete the contents of existing files.
wb+	Open file for reading and writing. Creates a new file if the file does not exist. Deletes contents of existing file.
ab+	Open file for reading and writing. Creates a new file if the file does not exist. Writes at the end of existing file.

Here are some examples on reading and writing binary data.

In this program, we will use the function *fwrite()* that can write complete structure variables at once to the file. The syntax of this function is:

```
fwrite(address_of_data, size_of_data, number_of_data_items, file_pointer)
```

Program# 78

Write binary data to file

```
#include <stdio.h>
#include <stdlib.h>

typedef struct
{
  char name[50];
  char gender[10];
  int age;
} employee;
```

```c
int main()
{
    FILE *file;
    employee emp;

    /* open file for writing in binary mode */
    file = fopen("test.dat", "wb");

    if (file == NULL)

    {
        printf("Cannot open the file");
        exit(0);
    }
    printf("Enter name: ");
    scanf("%[^\n]", emp.name);

    printf("Enter age: ");
    scanf("%d", &emp.age);

    /* clear enter key */
    getchar();

    printf("Enter gender (male/female/other): ");
    scanf("%s", emp.gender);

    printf("Now writing data to file\n");

    fwrite(&emp, sizeof(emp), 1, file);

    fclose(file);

    printf("\nData writing complete");

    return 0;
}
```

Run this program.

Now we will read data written to file by above program.

Here, we will use the function *fread()* that can read complete structure variables at once from the file. It returns the number of records it read. The syntax of this function is:

```
fread(address_of_data, size_of_data, number_of_data_items, file_pointer)
```

Program# 79

Read binary data from file

```c
#include <stdio.h>
#include <stdlib.h>

typedef struct
{
    char name[50];
    char gender[10];
    int age;
} employee;

int main()
{
    FILE *file;
    employee emp;

    /* open file for reading in binary mode */
    file = fopen("test.dat", "rb");

    if (file == NULL)
    {
        printf("Cannot open the file");
        exit(0);
    }

    printf("Reading data from file\n");

    fread(&emp, sizeof(emp), 1, file);
    printf("\nName: %s", emp.name);
    printf("\nAge: %d", emp.age);
    printf("\nGender: %s", emp.gender);

    fclose(file);

    printf("\nData reading complete");

    return 0;

}
```

Run this program.

Making copy of an existing file

In the next program, we will try to create a copy of an existing file. We will read bytes from one file and write to another file. To make our program efficient, we will use a buffer to read and write multiple bytes at once. We can choose whatever size of buffer we want.

Here is the program:

Program# 80

Make a copy of an existing file

```c
#include <stdio.h>
#include <stdlib.h>

#define SIZE 1024

int main()
{
   FILE *file_read, *file_write;
   int buffer[SIZE];
   int bytes;

   /* open file for reading in binary mode */
   file_read = fopen("first_file", "rb");

   if (file_read == NULL)
   {
      printf("Cannot open file to read");
      exit(0);
   }

   /* open file for writing in binary mode */
   file_write = fopen("second_file", "wb");

   if (file_write == NULL)
   {
      printf("Cannot open file to write");
      exit(0);
   }

   /* feof() function detects end of file */
   while (!feof(file_read))
```

```
{
    /* Read SIZE number of bytes */
    /* Actual count of bytes read is returned in variable bytes */
    bytes = fread(buffer, 1, SIZE, file_read);

    /* Write bytes number of bytes to output file */
    fwrite(buffer, 1, bytes, file_write);
}

fclose(file_read);
fclose(file_write);

printf("\nFile copy complete");

return 0;
}
```

Run this program.

UNSOLVED PROBLEMS

Q.1. Why should we use binary files? What are the problems with text files?

Q.2. Can we write any type of data to a binary file?

Q.3. What is the difference between ab+ and wb+ file modes?

Q.4. Why are we using pointers for opening files?

UNSOLVED PROGRAMS

Q.1. Write a program to store marks of 5 students in a file. Now, read the file back and find the student with highest marks. Consider 100 as the maximum marks for each subject. Use two structures with following fields:

```
struct marks
- subject_name
- marks

struct student
- rollno
- name
- marks
```

Q.2. Write a program to split a file into specified number of parts. Write another program to join the split files into one.

Q.3. Write a program to encode and decode a text file. You can create your own rule for encoding or decoding. Here is a sample rule:
Replace each entered character by another character in cyclic order,
For example:

```
a => d,
b => e...,
y => b,
z => c..
```

Hence, a string entered by user:

India is big

will become

Logld lv elj

Q.4. Read a text file and print word count of each line. The output looks like this:

```
Line 1: Count = 9
Line 2: Count = 12
Line 3: Count = 10
```

Q.5. Write a program to search for a word in a file and print its location. The output looks like this:

```
Enter word to search: India
India found at position 24
```

Q.6. Write a program to add data of employees to a file using structure. Now, find employee(s) by their id and post name. Following are the fields/variables of employees:

```
id, name, gender, post_name
```

CHAPTER 12

DATA STRUCTURES

Introduction to data structure

Data structure is a way of storing and retrieving data in an efficient manner. The purpose of data structure is:

1. Fast data storage
2. Fast data retrieval
3. Efficient memory management
4. Dynamic memory allocation
5. Memory management for new and deleted items

There are many data structures available to use based on our requirements. Here are some of the data structures we will see:

Stack

A stack is a data structure which works on the principle of *LIFO* (last in first out). The elements of the stack are always accessed by a variable named *top*. We can only access the top element of a stack and no other element can be accessed. Removing a value from the top is called *pop* whereas adding value at the top is called *push*.

A stack of the following numbers is given below:

```
1  4  7  12  5  6
```

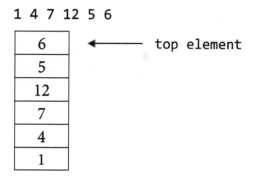

So, the numbers will be removed from the stack in the order:

```
6 5 12 7 4 1
```

Let us write a program to demonstrate the working of a stack.

Program# 81

Demonstrate the working of a stack

```c
#include<stdio.h>

#define MAX 10

int top = -1;
int stack[MAX];

int pop();
int push(int);
void show_stack();
void create_stack();
int is_stack_full();
int is_stack_empty();

int main()
{
    create_stack();
    show_stack();

    return 0;
}

void create_stack()
{
    int value;

    printf("Enter positive numbers, -1 to quit\n ");

    while(1)
    {
        if(is_stack_full())
        {
            printf("Stack is full...");
            break;
        }
```

```
        scanf("%d", &value);

        /* If input number is -1, stop reading more numbers */
        if(value == -1)
                break;

        push(value);
    }
}

void show_stack()
{
    printf("\nNow printing stack values…\n");
    while(1)
    {
        if(is_stack_empty())
        {
                printf("Stack is empty…");
                break;
        }

        printf("%d\n", stack[top--]);
    }
}

int is_stack_full()
{
    return top == MAX - 1;
}

int is_stack_empty()
{
    return top == -1;
}

int push(int value)
{
        stack[++top] = value;
}
```

```
int pop()
{
    return stack[top--];
}
```

Run this program.

Queue

A queue is a data structure that works on the principle of *FIFO* (first in first out). There are two variables associated with a queue: *front* that indicates the position of first element of the queue and *rear* that indicates the position of the last inserted element.

A queue of the following numbers is given below:

1 4 7 12 5 6

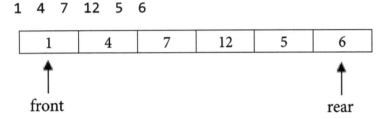

front   rear

The numbers will be removed in the order they were inserted.

1 4 7 12 5 6

Let us write a program to demonstrate the working of a queue.

Program# 82

Demonstrate the working of a queue

```
#include<stdio.h>

#define MAX 10

int queue[MAX];
int front = 0, rear = -1;

int dequeue();
void enqueue(int);
void show_queue();
void create_queue();
```

```c
int is_queue_full();
int is_queue_empty();

int main()
{
    create_queue();
    show_queue();

    return 0;
}

void create_queue()
{
    int value;
    printf("Enter positive numbers, -1 to quit\n");

    while(1)
    {
        if(is_queue_full())
        {
            printf("Queue is full");
            break;
        }

        scanf("%d", &value);

        if(value > -1)
            enqueue(value);
        else
            break;
    }
}

void show_queue()
{
    printf("Now printing queue values...\n");
    while(1)
    {
        if(is_queue_empty())
        {
            printf("Queue is empty");
            break;
        }
```

```
        printf("%d\n", dequeue());
   }
}
int is_queue_empty()
{
   return rear == -1;
}

int is_queue_full()
{
   return rear == MAX;
}

void enqueue(int value)
{
   queue[++rear] = value;
}

int dequeue()
{
   int value = queue[front++];

   if(front > rear)
      front = rear = -1;

   return value;
}
```

Run this program.

Deque

A deque or double ended queue is a special version of queue that allows insertion and deletion of data on both ends. A deque uses two positional variables *front* and *rear* to manage its elements.

To insert and delete values from deque, we need to follow these rules:

1. Add to front => front = front – 1
2. Add to rear => rear = rear + 1

3. Overflow when rear = MAX – 1 or front = 0
4. Delete from front => front = front + 1
5. Delete from rear => rear = rear – 1
6. Cannot delete from rear when front = rear or rear = -1
7. Cannot delete from front when front = rear

We are going to maintain following 3 variables:

1. *MAX* which represents maximum number of elements in the deque
2. *front* which represents the position of front element
3. *rear* which represents the position of rear element

Step 1: Initialize variables

$$MAX = 6$$
$$front = -1$$
$$rear = -1$$

Step 2: Insert 1 at rear

$$front = 0$$
$$rear = rear + 1 = 0$$

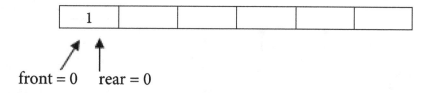

Step 3: Insert 4 at rear

$$front = 0$$
$$rear = rear + 1 = 1$$

Step 4: Insert 7 at rear

$$front = 0$$
$$rear = rear + 1 = 2$$

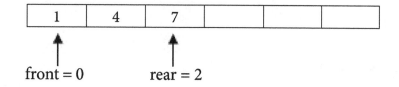

Step 5: Insert 12 at rear

        front = 0

        rear = rear + 1 = 3

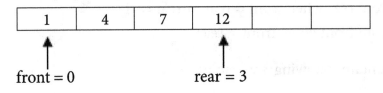

Step 6: Delete from front

        front = front + 1 = 1

        rear = rear 3

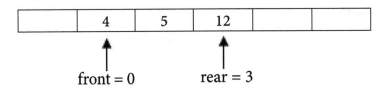

Step 7: Delete from rear

        front = 1

        rear = rear - 1 = 2

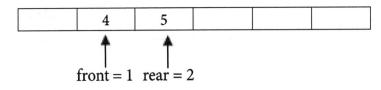

Step 8: Insert 10 at front

        front = front − 1 = 0

        rear = 2

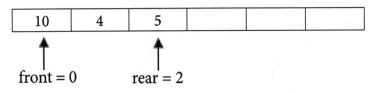

Following are the functions we can use to work with a deque. Try to create your own program on deque using these functions.

```
int is_empty()
{
    return rear == -1;
}

void insert_front(int value)
```

```c
{
   /* Check if space available */
   if(front <= 0)
      printf("\nNo space available");
   else
   {
      front = front - 1;
      deque[front] = value;
   }
}

void insert_rear(int value)
{
   /* Check if space available */
   if (rear == MAX - 1)
      printf("\No space available");
   else
   {
      rear = rear + 1;
      deque[rear] = value;
   }
}

void delete_front()
{
   /* Check if deque is empty */
   if(is_empty())
   {
      printf("\nNo more elements to delete");
      return;
   }

   printf("\n%d removed", deque[front]);

   /* Deque has only one element */
   if (front == rear)
   {
      front = -1;
      rear = -1;
   }
```

```
    else
        front = front + 1;
}

void delete_rear()
{
    /* Check if deque is empty */
    if(is_empty())
    {
        printf("\nNo more elements to delete");
        return;
    }

    printf("\n%d removed", deque[rear]);

    /* Deque has only one element */
    if (front == rear)
    {
        front = -1;
        rear = -1;
    }
    else
        rear = rear - 1;
}
```

Linked list

A linked list is a linear data structure in which elements are not stored at contiguous (one after another) memory like in array. This allows us to manage memory for elements dynamically.

Hence we can say where memory management is a priority, linked list are preferred over arrays.

The elements in the linked list are connected in a single direction by a *next* pointer. For this, we need to use self-referential structures as we saw earlier. Here is an example of a structure that can be used to represent an element in a linked list:

```
typedef struct linked_list_node
{
    int data;
    struct node *next;
} node;
```

The name of the structure is *linked_list_node* here and its short name is *node*.

Each element/memory in a linked list is called a node. The first node of the linked list is generally called the *root node*.

> **Note**
>
> The variable data is here used for example; we can have any number or type of variables we want.

To work with a linked list, we need to store the first node in some root variable. Then we traverse the linked list nodes by using the *next* pointer of every node.

Following are the operations performed on a linked list:

1. Create
2. Insert
3. Read
4. Search
5. Insert
6. Delete

1. Create

To create a linked list, we need to first initialize a starting node and set its value. Here is a function that can be used to create a linked list:

```c
node* create_list()
{
    node *start = (node*)malloc(sizeof(node));

    printf("\nCreating linked list");
    printf("\nEnter data: ");
    scanf("%d", &start->data);

    start->next = NULL;

    printf("\nList created");

    return start;
}
```

2. Read

We can use the following function to read the full linked list:

```c
void read_linked_list(node* root)
{
    node* current_node = root;

    /* Read the linked list unless the node is NULL */
    while( current_node != NULL)
    {
        printf("\n%d", current_node->data);

        /* move to the next node */
        currrent_node = current_node->next;
    }
}
```

3. Search

We can use the following function to search for an item in the linked list:

```c
void search_value(node* root, int value_to_search)
{
    int found = 0;
    int position = 0;
    node* current_node = root;

    /* Read the linked list unless the node is NULL */
    while( current_node != NULL)
    {
        ++position;

        if( current_node->data == value_to_search)
        {
            printf("\n%d found at position %d", current_node->data, position);
            found = 1;
        }

        /* move to the next node */
        currrent_node = current_node->next;
    }
}
```

4. Insert

Here is the 216 list:

Ask the user when s/he wants to insert the new node.

Case 1: Insert a new node in the beginning

   a. Create the new node
   b. Set the root node as next of the new node
   c. Set the new node as the root node

Case 2: Insert after a given node

   a. To insert a node in the middle (let us call it *new_node*), first we need to move to the node after which we need to insert the new node (let us call it *current_node*)
   b. Next we copy *current_node->next* in a *temporary_node*
   c. Next *current_node->next = new_node*
   d. Next *new_node->next = temporary_node*

Case 3: Insert at the end

   a. To insert a node (let us call it *new_node*) at the end of the list, we first move to the last node of the linked list (let us call it *current_node*)
   b. Next *new_node->next* = NULL
   c. Next *current_node->next = new_node*

Here is the complete function for inserting an element in a linked list:

```c
void insert_node(node* root, int value_to_search)
{
    int found = 0;
    int position = 0;
    node* current_node = root;

    /* Read the linked list unless the node is NULL */
    while( current_node != NULL)
    {
        ++position;
        if(current_node->data == value_to_search)
        {
            printf("\n%d found at position %d", current_node->data, position);
            found = 1;
        }
```

```
        /* move to the next node */
        currrent_node = current_node->next;
    }
}
```

5. Delete

Here is the process of deleting a node from the list:
Search the node to be deleted by checking its value.

Case 1: The search matches the first node, means delete the first node

> a. Copy the root node to a temporary node (let us call it *temporary_node*)
> b. Do *temporary_node = root*
> c. Next *root = root->next*
> d. Now delete *temporary_node*

Case 2: We need to delete node other than the first node

> a. First move to the node just before the last node of the linked list (let us call it *current_node*)
> b. Next *node_to_delete = current_node->next*
> c. Next *current_node->next = node_to_delete->next*
> d. Delete *node_to_delete*

Here is the complete function for deleting an element from the linked list:

```c
void delete_node(node* root, int value_to_search)
{
    int found = 0;
    int position = 0;
    node* current_node = root;

    /* Read the linked list unless the node is NULL */
    while( current_node != NULL)
    {
        ++position;

        if(current_node->data == value_to_search)
        {
            printf("\n%d found at position %d", current_node->data, position);
            found = 1;
        }
```

```c
    /* move to the next node */
    currrent_node = current_node->next;
  }
}
```

Program# 83

Demonstrate the working of a linked list

```c
#include<stdio.h>
#include<stdlib.h>

typedef struct link_list_node
{
    int data;
    struct link_list_node *next;
} node;

int menu();
void search_node();
void insert_node();
void delete_node();
void create_list();
void display_list();

node *start;

int main()
{
    int choice;
    node *temp;

    while (1)
    {
        choice = menu();

        switch (choice) {

        case 1:
                create_list();
                break;
```

```c
        case 2:
            insert_node();
            break;

        case 3:
            delete_node();
            break;

        case 4:

            search_node();
            break;

        case 5:
            display_list();
            break;

        case 6:
            printf("\nExiting");
            exit(0);

        default:
            printf("Invalid choice");
            break;
        }
    }
}

int menu()
{
    int choice;

    printf("\n\nLinked List Menu");
    printf("\n\n1. Create list");
    printf("\n2. Add node to list");
    printf("\n3. Delete node from list");
    printf("\n4. Search node in list");
    printf("\n5. Display the list");
    printf("\n6. Quit");

    printf("\nEnter your choice: ");
    scanf("%d", &choice);
```

```c
    return choice;
}

void create_list()
{
    start = (node*) malloc(sizeof (node));

    printf("\nCreating linked list");
    printf("\nEnter data: ");
    scanf("%d", &start->data);

    start->next = NULL;

    printf("\nList created");
}

void display_list()
{
    int count = 0;
    node *current_node = start;

    if (start == NULL)
    {
        printf("\nList is empty");
        return;
    }

    printf("\nDisplaying list contents\n");

    while (current_node != NULL)
    {
        ++count;
        printf("\n%d. %d", count, current_node->data);
        current_node = current_node->next;
    }
}

void search_node()
{
    int value;
    int count = 0;
    int found = 0;
```

```c
    node *current_node = start;

    if (start == NULL)
    {
        printf("\nList is empty");
        return;
    }

    printf("\nSearching list contents\n");

    printf("Enter value to search: ");
    scanf("%d", &value);

    while (current_node != NULL)
    {
        ++count;

        if (current_node->data == value)
        {
            found = 1;
            printf("\n%d found at position %d", current_node->data, count);
        }

        current_node = current_node->next;
    }

    if (found == 0)

        printf("\n%d not found in list", value);
}

void insert_node()
{
    int count;
    int position;
    int found = 0;
    node *new_node, *current_node, *temp;

    printf("\nAdding node to list");
    printf("\nEnter node number after which to add new node (0 for start): ");
    scanf("%d", &position);

    new_node = (node*) malloc(sizeof (node));
```

```
    printf("Enter data: ");
    scanf("%d", &new_node->data);

    if (position == 0)
    {
        new_node->next = start;
        start = new_node;

        printf("\nNode added to list");
    }
    else
    {
        current_node = start;

        count = 0;
        while (current_node != NULL)
        {
            ++count;

            if (position == count)
            {
                temp = current_node->next;
                current_node->next = new_node;
                new_node->next = temp;

                found = 1;
                break;
            }

            current_node = current_node->next;
        }

        if (found == 0)
            printf("%d position not found in the list", position);
        else
            printf("\nNode added to list");
    }
}

void delete_node()
{
    int value;
```

```c
int found = 0;

node *temp;
node *current_node = start;

printf("\nDeleting a node");
printf("\nEnter value you want to delete: ");
scanf("%d", &value);

if (start == NULL)
{
    printf("\nList is empty");
    return;
}

/* check if we need to delete first node */
if (start->data == value)
{
    /* check if there are any other nodes */
    if (start->next != NULL)
    {
        start = current_node->next;
        free(current_node);

        printf("\n%d deleted from list", value);
        return;
    }
    else
    {
        /* This is the only node */
        free(current_node);
        start = NULL;
        printf("\n%d deleted from list", value);
        return;
    }
}
else
{
    while (current_node->next != NULL)
    {
        if (current_node->next->data == value)
```

```
            {
                temp = current_node->next;
                current_node->next = temp->next;
                free(temp);
                found = 1;

                printf("\n%d deleted from list", value);
                break;
            }

            current_node = current_node->next;
        }
    }

    if (found == 0)
        printf("\n%d not found in list", value);
}
```

Run this program.

Doubly linked list

A doubly linked list is a linked list with data fields and two pointers: *previous* and *next*. As the name suggests, the *previous* pointer represents the previous node in the list whereas the *next* pointer represents the next node in the list.

The first node of a doubly linked has *previous = NULL* whereas the last node has *next = NULL*. tructure for a double linked list can be written like this:

```
typedef struct
{
    int data;
    struct node *next;
    struct node *previous;
} node;
```

Tree

A tree is a hierarchical representation of data stored in nodes. It is a non-linear data structure in which the starting node is called the root node. All other nodes are called child nodes of root. Here is how a tree looks like:

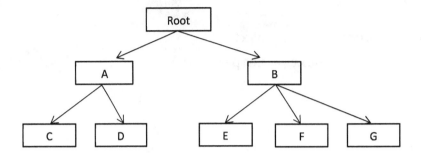

Following are the terms associated with a tree:

1. **Root**

   This is the first node in the tree.

2. **Parent**

   Each node other than the root node has a parent. Parent of D is A, parent of F is B etc.

3. **Sub tree**

   A sub tree represents children of a node. For example, the root contains two sub-trees containing elements: A, C, D and B, E, F, G

4. **Child**

   A connected node below any given node is called child of that node. For example, E is child node of B.

5. **Leaf**

   A node having no child node is called a leaf node or a terminal node. In the above given tree: C, D, E, F, G are the leaf nodes.

6. **Edge**

   Line connecting two nodes is called an edge.

7. **Path**

   A path represents the sequence of nodes from root to a given node. For example:
   Root -> B -> F

8. **Level**

   The level of a node is defined by the number of nodes between the node and the root node of the tree + 1. For example:

   Level of node A is 0 + 1 = 1   , no node between A and Root
   Level of node C is 1 + 1 = 2   , one node (A) between C and Root

9. **Height**

   Height of a tree is the maximum level of any node in the tree. The height of above tree is 2.

Binary tree

A binary tree is a tree where each node can have a maximum of two child nodes. The two children are called left node and right node. An example of a binary tree is:

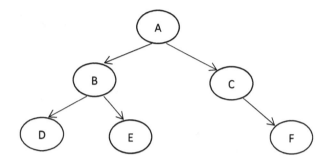

We can use following structure to represent a binary tree:

```
typedef struct tree_data
{
    int data;
    struct tree_data *left;
    struct tree_data *right;
} tree;
```

Binary search tree (BST)

A binary search tree is a special case of binary tree in which the value of left node is always less than its parent whereas the value of right node is always greater than the parent node.

Here is an example of a binary tree:

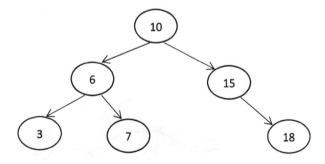

Binary search tree creation

Let we have following values from which we need to create a binary search tree:

```
10  6  15  3  7  18
```

Here are the steps:

Step 1: First value as root

Step 2: 6 < 10

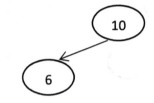

Step 3: 15 > 10

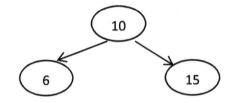

Step 4: 3 < 10, 3 < 6

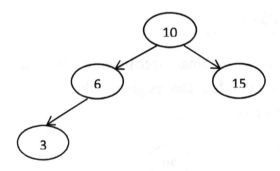

Step 5: 7 < 10, 7 > 6

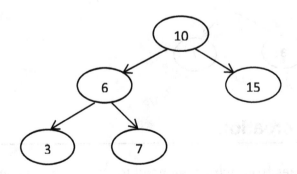

Step 6:   18 > 10, 18 > 15

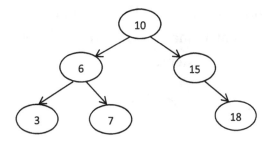

Binary tree traversal

Traversing the tree means visiting each node of the tree in some defined order. Tree traversal can be done in three ways:

1. **Pre-order traversal**

    In this traversal, root is visited first, then left sub-tree is traversed and finally the right sub-tree is traversed. For the following tree, here are the traversal steps:

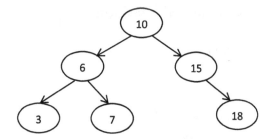

```
Visit 10:        10    6      15
Visit 6:         10    6      3     7      15
Visit 15:        10    6      3     7      15     18
```

Here is a function to traverse a BST in pre-order fashion:

```c
void preorder_traversal(tree *node)
{
    if(node != NULL)
    {
        printf("%d\t", node->data);
        preorder_traversal(node->left);
        preorder_traversal(node->right);
    }
}
```

2. **In-order traversal**

In this traversal, first left sub-tree is traversed, then root is visited and finally the right sub-tree is traversed. In-order traversal of a binary search tree will always give us sorted result. For the following tree, here are the traversal steps:

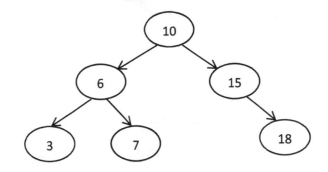

```
Visit 10:       6     10    15
Visit 6:        3     6     7     10    15
Visit 15:       3     6     7     10    15    18
```

Here is a function to traverse a BST in in-order fashion:

```c
void inorder_traversal(tree *node)
{
    if(node != NULL)
    {
        inorder_traversal(node->left);
        printf("%d\t", node->data);
        inorder_traversal(node->right);
    }
}
```

3. **Post-order traversal**

In this traversal, left sub-tree is traversed first, then right sub-tree is traversed and finally the root is visited. For the following tree, here are the traversal steps:

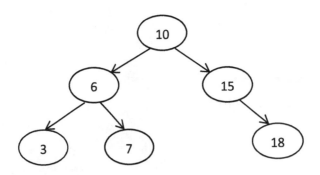

```
Visit 10:        6     15    10
Visit 6:         3     7     6     15    10
Visit 15:        3     7     6     18    15    10
```

Here is a function to traverse a BST in post-order fashion:

```
void postorder_traversal(tree *node)
{
    if(node != NULL)
    {
        postorder_traversal(node->left);
        postorder_traversal(node->right);
        printf("%d\t", node->data);
    }
}
```

Binary search tree insertion and deletion

Insertion

Values are always inserted as leaves in a binary search tree. The position of new value in a binary search tree depends on the value itself, as we need to compare it the value of root node. For example, if we want to insert 14 in above tree, we will make following steps:

1. Compare 14 with 10, since 14 > 10, we move to right side of 10
2. Compare 14 with 15, since 14 < 15, we move to left of 15
3. Since 15 has no left sub tree, we place 14 on left of 15

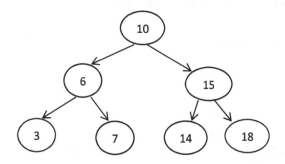

```
tree* insert(tree* node, int key)
{
    /* If the tree is empty, return a new node */
    if (node == NULL)
```

```
{
    tree *temp = (tree*)malloc(sizeof(tree));
    temp->data = key;
    temp->left = temp->right = NULL;
    return temp;
}

/* Otherwise, move down the tree and repeat */
if (key < node->data)
    node->left = insert(node->left, key);
else
    node->right = insert(node->right, key);

/* return the originally passed node */

return node;
}
```

Deletion

Deletion is not as straight forward as creation and insertion. It requires re-structuring the tree. There are two cases when deleting a node in a binary tree:

1. **Deleting a leaf**

    To delete a leaf, we just need to set its parent left or right node to NULL. For example, if we want to delete 3, we just have to set left of node with value 6 to NULL.

2. **Deleting a node with children**

    To delete a node with children, we have to move one of the nodes as its replacement. For this, we need to find the in-order successor of the node to be deleted.

    To understand it better, first we will traverse the tree in in-order fashion:

    ```
    3    6    7    10    14    15    18
    ```

Delete 15:

The node with value 15 has child nodes; so we need to find in-order successor of 15 which is 18. The resultant tree after deleting 15 will be:

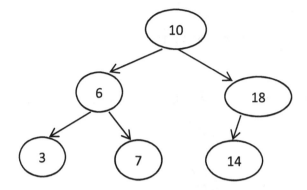

Delete 10:

The node with value 10 has child nodes; so we need to find the in-order successor of 10 which is 14. The resultant tree after deleting 10 will be:

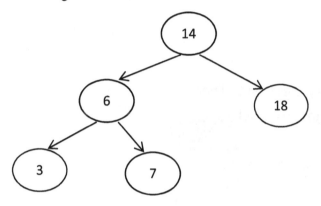

Here is a function that can be used to delete a node from BST. Pass the root node and key to be deleted to this function:

```
tree* delete_node(tree *node, int key)
{
    if (node == NULL) return node;
    /*
        If the key to be deleted is smaller than the node's key,
        then it lies in left sub-tree
    */
    if (key < node->data)
        node->left = delete_node(node->left, key);

    /*
    If the key to be deleted is greater than the node's key,
    then it lies in the right sub-tree
    */
```

```c
        else if (key > node->data)
            node->right = delete_node(node->right, key);

        /*
        If key is same as node's value, then this is the node to be deleted
        */
        else
        {
            /* If node has only right sub tree */
            if (node->left == NULL)
            {
                tree *temp = node->right;
                free(node);
                return temp;
            }

            /* If node has only left sub tree */
            else if (node->right == NULL)
            {
                tree *temp = node->left;
                free(node);
                return temp;
            }

            /*
            Node has both child, get in-order successor in the right sub tree
            */
            tree *temp = get_inorder_successor(node->right);

            /* Copy the in-order successor's value to this node */
            node->data = temp->data;

            /* Delete the in-order successor */
            node->right = delete_node(node->right, temp->data);
        }

        return node;
    }
```

Heap Introduction

A heap is a special binary tree in which the parent of the sub-tree follows any of the following two conditions:

1. **Min-Heap**

    In this kind of heap, the value of the root node is less than or equal to the values of any of its child nodes.

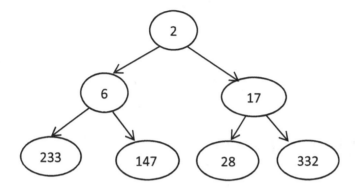

2. **Max-Heap**

    In this kind of heap, the value of the parent node is greater than or equal to the values of its child nodes.

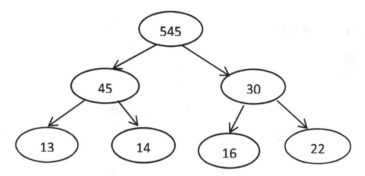

Max-Heap creation

Building max-heap requires two steps:

1. Create a binary tree by simply adding elements

2. Update this tree values to convert it into a heap (process is called heapify)

Let we have following values from which we need to create a binary search tree:

```
10  12  11  3  17  14
```

Here are the steps:

Step 1: First value as root

Step 2: Second value is 12, insert at left of 10

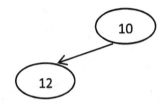

Step 3: Next value is 11, insert at right of 10

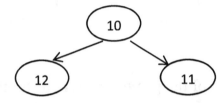

Step 4: Next value is 3, insert at left of 12

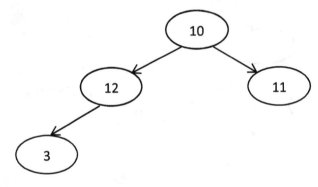

Step 5: Next value is 7, insert at right of 12

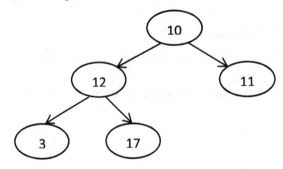

Step 6: Next value is 18, insert at left of 11

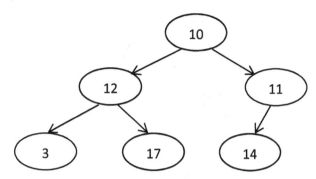

Now, we need to update values of the above tree (heapify) to convert it into a heap.

For this, we will first swap biggest value in parent of sub-trees with leaves and repeat the process in upward direction.

Here are the steps:

Step 1: Heapify sub-tree with nodes 12, 3, 17

Swap 12 with 17 as 17 is the biggest value

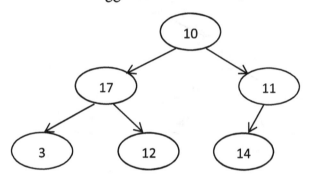

Step 2: Heapify sub-tree with nodes 11, 14

Swap 11 with 14 as 14 is the bigger value

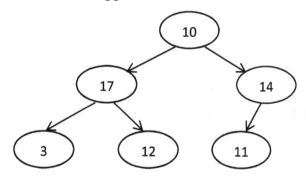

Step 3: Heapify sub-tree with nodes 10, 17, 14

Swap 10 with 17 as 17 is the biggest value

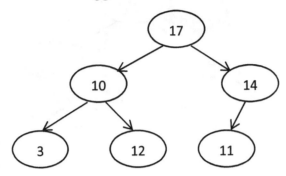

But we can clearly see, the sub-tree 10, 3, 12 is not following the max-heap property. For this, we need to heapify this sub-tree as well.

Step 4: Heapify sub-tree with nodes 10, 3, 12

Swap 12 with 10 as 12 is the biggest value

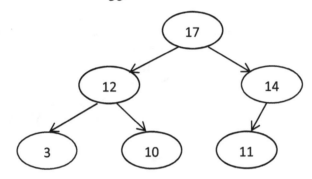

The max-heap is ready now.

Similarly, try to create min-heap on your own.

UNSOLVED PROBLEMS

Q.1. What is a balanced binary tree?

Q.2. How can we search a value in binary search tree?

Q.3. How can we search a value in binary search tree?